The Age of Sage

Extraordinary Advice for Extraordinary Women

Judith Pepper

Copyright © 2012 by Judith Pepper

All rights reserved. No part of this publication may be reproduced without permission, stored in a retrieval system or transmitted in any form or by any means, electronic, mechanical, photocopying, recording or otherwise without prior written permission from the copyright owner.

ISBN 13: 978-0-9815509-2-3
ISBN 10: 0-9815509-2-4

Published by Kora Press
www.KoraPress.com
New York, NY: 2012
Printed in the United States of America

KORA
PRESS

The Age of Sage

You can imagine my complete bewilderment when I was doodling with graphic designs for my website when I used the first letters of each word of The Age of Sage, to create a design and the word "TAOS" appeared on my paper. Literally, the name of my business and website spelled "Taos!" Having lived and worked in Taos for ten years and experienced its highly charged spirituality, its history, the Hispanic and Native American cultures, I realized naming my business was totally out of my human experience and fashioned by the Muses and Angels from Northern New Mexico.

Judith Pepper

Acknowledgements

*E*very page in this book was written with an experience or a person in mind. Some will be recognized in this acknowledgement and some will not to protect us both! Without the Friends of Bill W. and my Higher Power I would be nothing, much less have had the discipline or the interest to write.

I particularly want to thank the people who have supported me in my endeavor to write this book—Mary Coyne, Ellen Robertson Green, Ivette Principe, Melanie Erickson, Dorla Whitman Belz, Kathy Hall, Daniel Bayless, Dow Kee and my sister, Joan Hodge. Each of you held the space between self-doubt and self-love and inspired me to complete the task.

I am grateful to Joanna Francis, Kora Press publisher who has been gentle, kind and firm as she guided me with the manuscript to the finished product.

Lastly, I want to thank you, the reader. Writing a book is much like a tree falling in the forest. If no one hears the tree fall, there is no noise. If no one reads my book, there is no book. My hope is you are inspired from the first page to the last.

Introduction

OKAY, I KNOW. PEOPLE WRITE books all the time. What is this book about? It is about me. It is about you. It is about how life starts and stops in 15 second increments and the pain and joy that come in the gap. Oh yeah, you are thinking this is another self-help book. Well, get down from the ceiling and believe me when I say, this is not a self-help book.

This book is inspirational: I was inspired to write it, and you are seeking inspiration to ignite your passions. My inspiration comes from my spiritual connection to a Spirit that doesn't conform to any religion. I have a very strong faith in a Power greater than myself. My faith in this Power has propelled me through addiction and recovery, marriage and divorce, moving from home and family to large and small communities, changing jobs more than I care to admit. It takes courage to change, embrace your bold self and move out of a comfort zone that feels safe.

I'm Judith Pepper, an extraordinary woman with extraordinary life experiences. I've won blue ribbons in competitions and on occasion I have placed second. Both positions provide a perspective of living life on life's terms. I have a very personal perspective of women and the demons that haunt them.

I am the youngest of five children, both my parents are deceased and I have a multitude of friends from every walk of life. I have no children and that was a conscious decision I made early in my life, with no regrets!

I've lived in rural communities and the metropolitan city of Houston. The most enchanting spot I've lived in is Taos, New Mexico, where I worked on Taos Pueblo, managing millions of dollars in grants for the Taos Pueblo Tribe. I oversaw the development and implementation of a nonprofit agency that built the Internet in Northern New Mexico, won two national awards and skied as much as I could on brilliant sunny days on Taos Mountain, before snowboards! My professional background is nonprofit management with community based organizations.

My first speaking engagement was in ninth grade Speech and Drama class and I made an F. However, I adored being on stage and engaging the audience. If the teacher had let me do stand up comedy, I would have aced the class! But alas, I had to wait twenty years to begin telling stories to enchant audiences with my *joie de vivre*.

I have a calling with Spirit. I am transfixed daily with a message of love coming from my Higher Power, when I am befuddled and filled with angst. I was introduced to this Power as a little girl while lying in the grass with the breeze blowing through leaves, when I knew there was something holding me safely and securely. This relationship blossomed on the day I surrender to addiction.

Introduction

For the past 27 years I have explored the relationship between recovery from addiction and spiritual principles and have devised formulas that complement the two. I share these formulas with you to transform your desires to reality!

My journey of living life with spiritual principles began on August 25th, 1984. The ride has been excruciating at times. I have resisted the messengers sent to protect me and twisted the message. I am not sure when I surrendered totally, but I know that in the past seven years I have come to understand the death urge that comes with transition and that my life struggles are less intense and less important. I have found peace and enjoy life in ways that boggle my imagination.

I am happy.

What am I offering you?
I've experienced living life on my terms as well as on others' terms, and life on my terms is best. I understand humanity is a dynamic force that requires compassion, understanding and love. My spiritual life sustains me. I live by 12 spiritual principles. I strive to be the best me I can be through prayer and meditation. I am in constant transition as I abhor stagnation.

You are invited to open this book to any page and be inspired to live a bigger life. Whatever religion or spirituality you practice that offers you community and support will not be challenged by the spiritual principles I refer to in this book. Not every narrative I have written will reveal a specific spiritual principle, but every narrative

The Age of Sage

is based on one.

One of my favorite life changing quotes is, "I'd rather be comfortable than build my character." In the past I have had grand ideas and visions that required taking action and getting out of my comfort zone. I was fearful and the fear masked as comfort was procrastination and resistance to taking action. Being bold requires character. Building your dream requires character. Be comfortable later, or at least not every day. Grab hold of life, be bold and live a life of joy and adventure. Be the author of your life.

This book is a direct result of the perfect timing in my life and the encouragement from friends and family and in particular a psychic, whom you will meet in the book. The book is divided into the twelve months of a year, with four narratives for each month, offering advice on a myriad of circumstances. Some of the advice will resonate with you, some of it may make you laugh, perhaps even cry. Hopefully it will enhance your life, just by you implementing the spiritual principle or idea.

Whatever the result, I hope you have fun and we can meet along the way.

"Whatever you can do or dream you can, begin it. Boldness has genius, magic and power in it. Begin it now."
Johann Wolfgang von Goethe

The Age of Sage: Contents

January
Forging ahead with new ideas or starting over after disappointing failures... Page 15
✳ Beginnings.. Page 17
✳ The Game of Life and How to Play It......... Page 20
✳ Decisions... Page 23
✳ Heart's Desires... Page 25

February
Romance, love, friendship and family........................ Page 29
✳ Valentine's Day... Page 31
✳ Friends... Page 34
✳ I Love You... Page 37
✳ My Bold Family.. Page 39

March
Inspiring actions.. Page 43
✳ I'm Not Inspired Today................................ Page 45
✳ Blahsville... Page 47
✳ No Safety Nets!... Page 50
✳ Alphabet Spirituality.................................... Page 54

April
The joy of simplistic living... Page 57
✳ I Left the Bed Unmade................................ Page 59
✳ Simplistic Living.. Page 61
✳ Life—Simplistic or Austere?....................... Page 63
✳ Thank-You Notes... Page 67

May
*Invitations to enjoy finance, money,
prosperity and abundance*... Page 69
✱ The Value of Education............................... Page 71
✱ Prosperity and Abundance.......................... Page 73
✱ Money Magic... Page 77
✱ Life Rewards.. Page 80

June
Healthy living.. Page 83
✱ Make Dining Fun!....................................... Page 85
✱ Healthy Dining... Page 88
✱ "Use It or Lose It"....................................... Page 90
✱ What's Your Pleasure?................................. Page 92

July
Success... Page 97
✱ Mistakes Are Spirit in Action...................... Page 99
✱ Freedom... Page 101
✱ Take the Next Right Action........................ Page 103
✱ How to Thrive at Work............................... Page 106

August
The joy of giving and receiving................................. Page 109
✱ Buy the Raffle Ticket.................................. Page 111
✱ Smiling .... Page 114
✱ Receiving... Page 116
✱ Psychic Session... Page 118

The Age of Sage: Contents

September
Facing fears and finding the gift.............................. Page 123
✳ Finding Faith in Fear...................................... Page 125
✳ Faced My Fear of a Bridge Game................ Page 128
✳ Walking... Page 132
✳ Inspirations From Women............................ Page 134

October
Creating physical movement from the spiritual realm... Page 137
✳ Right Outcomes Are Unfolding.................... Page 139
✳ Action Is the Process .... Page 142
✳ Happiness... Page 146
✳ Reality Check.. Page 149

November
The simplistic tool of gratitude................................. Page 151
✳ Be Grateful No Matter What........................ Page 153
✳ Why a Gratitude List..................................... Page 157
✳ Thanksgiving... Page 160
✳ Create Your Desires in Silence,
   Imagination and Gratitude........................... Page 162

December
The holidays.. Page 165
✳ Christmas at My House................................. Page 167
✳ The Most Extraordinary Gift....................... Page 170
✳ All I Want for Christmas!.............................. Page 172
✳ The Gift That Keeps on Giving................... Page 173
✳ For the Fun of It!.. Page 175

January

Forging ahead with new ideas or starting over after disappointing failures

Beginnings

*H*APPY NEW YEAR. A NEW YEAR. Anything can happen. Possibilities abound. Or is it just another day, the day after December 31st? Do you celebrate New Year's Day? Will the New Year bring new beginnings or continued middles and endings?

January 1st is often seen as a day of reflections about the past year and possible manifestations for the year to come. Reviewing the evidence of successes and challenges suggests that I am living a bold life with as much pleasure and joy as possible, as well as humility and oftentimes an arrogance that even gives me cause to pause.

You may consider keeping a journal beginning January 1st, or any day for that matter, to review each month or each year for outcomes of your desires. Do you know the desires of your heart? Is today a good day to pierce your desire bubble and let them drip easily and effortlessly onto the journal's pages?

Women often delay or do not know their heart's desires because they are overwhelmed with life circumstances. Family, work, home, school, community, health, children, husband, parents—each of these very real and very important circumstances exhaust the nature of self for

The Age of Sage

women, leaving little time to place importance on what we desire and require.

Taking time for yourself is vital. Like me, you have heard it a million times on Oprah, Good Morning America, The Today Show and Dr. Phil. If you are like me, you wanted to scream "Show me the time," like "Show me the money," because time and self simply did not compute in my world. If I took the time to take care of me, something or someone got out of whack, so the messages were loud, as was my fear. Finally out of frustration and pure desire, I stole a little time for myself and *voilá*, there was more of me to give, not less.

Get the journal, leave the guys to the football games, leave the kids with a snack and turn your cell phone to vibrate so the ringing calls don't interrupt your thoughts and start writing. Put the date at the top of the page. Write, "Desires of My Heart" and make a list of your heart's desires. Here is the caveat—the desires have to be about YOU, not your husband's job promotion, or your kid's college acceptance letter, or your mother's brain tumor.

A few examples to get you going:
- ♥ Hour and a half massage
- ♥ Monthly facials
- ♥ Once a week coffee date with someone who makes you laugh
- ♥ More time for myself
- ♥ Dozens of red roses
- ♥ Kitchen remodel
- ♥ Half hour for a bubble bath, with no

interruptions
- ♥ Sell this house and buy my dream house
- ♥ Wardrobe consultant
- ♥ Hot, steamy sex with my partner
- ♥ A surprise date with my guy
- ♥ A new car just for me.

Manifesting your heart's desires is the goal for this list. The best part is to let go and let them transpire from Spirit and the Universe. You will want to begin the journey for each of them by taking initial fact-finding steps, such as calling the spa and asking about the cost of a massage and facials. To really get the energy flowing make a hard copy of the desire list and post it on the refrigerator for all to see. When your guy or significant other asks you what you want for your birthday or a special day, offer this list for reference. Let him know which spa you desire to visit, which car has made your palms sweat, where you desire to have a romantic dinner.

Share your heart's desires with pleasure and juice and allow them to manifest easily and effortlessly. Bold desires result in bold living. Be bold.

The Game of Life and How to Play It

FLORENCE SCOVEL SHINN WAS an American artist and book illustrator who became a New Thought spiritual teacher and metaphysical author in the early 1900s. She wrote *The Game of Life and How to Play It* in 1925. Shinn believed in the power of thought and its influences on our lives. Believe and think positively, good follows; believe and think negatively, despair follows.

I was introduced to "Flo Sco" in 2006 when I enrolled in a class for women in New York City. Flo's life philosophy was not new to me as I had studied the teachings of Emmet Fox, a metaphysical teacher and author, for twenty years. Fox and Shinn were contemporaries, believing in and teaching the power of thought.

I live by New Thought and the metaphysic spiritual principles taught by Shinn and Fox. Listed on the next page are several of my favorite quotes from *The Game of Life and How to Play It*.* They resonate with me because of their power in creating the life I desire.

---

* Scovel Shinn, Florence. *The Game of Life and How to Play It.* DeVorss & Company. Camarillo, CA: 1978.

The Game of Life and How to Play It

❊ In Divine Mind, there is only completion, therefore my demonstration is complete: my perfect work, my perfect health, my perfect home, my perfect LOVE.

❊ I now smash and demolish, by my spoken word, every untrue record in my subconscious mind. It shall return to the dust-heap of its native nothingness, for it came from my own vain imaginings; I now make my perfect records through the Spirit within—the records of Health, Wealth, Love and Perfect Self Expression. This is the Square of Life, the Game completed.

❊ There is a place that I am to fill and no one else can fill, something I am to do, which no one else can do.

❊ I cannot lose anything that belongs to me by Divine Right. I am under grace and not under law.

❊ As one door shuts, another door opens.

❊ My ship comes in over a calm sea. Poise and nonresistance are power.

❊ I look with wonder at that which is before me.

These are powerful illustrations of positive thought and I challenge you to use the philosophy behind these statements to reframe and adjust areas in your life that are troublesome.

Are you experiencing financial problems? Relationship problems? Work problems? Health problems? Use one or all of these statements as a meditation and practice the positive and powerful thoughts behind the words. Better yet, I suggest you study the New Thought philosophy taught by Shinn and Fox and realize the bounty of positive thought.

Today, I look with wonder at that which is before me. I am amazed at my life circumstances. My finances are in order. My home is beautiful. My health is amazing. I am living my dream of perfect health, wealth and love. I live my perfect self-expression every day. Whatever comes up in the natural flow of events, I ask for what is rightfully mine from Divine Mind.

If these New Thought ideas are new to you, make a list of the life challenges you have identified. Using that list, sit quietly and invite Spirit to adjust the challenges to opportunities. State the opportunity and then say, "I look with wonder at that which is before me." Notice the change in your thoughts as you process the idea that the power of your spoken word can alter a challenge to an opportunity.

I have created romance, work, money, time, international travel invitations, gifts and more using metaphysical teachings of positive thinking. Successful demonstrations follow my new thoughts. Sometimes they happen quickly, sometimes slowly, but they always materialize when I focus on them with New Thought practices.

Infinite Spirit, don't let me miss a trick.

Decisions

"*WE MUST DECIDE WHAT we will not do, and then we can act with vigor in what we will do.*" (I cannot cite the author of this quote. I keep a file of quotes that resonate with me and this is one of them... should you know the author, please send the name and I will give credit where it is due.)

My friend Ruthie called this morning because she is confused in the midst of packing to return to California. She is undecided about whether the move is right, all while she is getting new tires on her truck. The moving truck is parked in her driveway ready for loading and a California friend has flown to Texas to help her move.

After she lamented the decision I asked her to identify her top three fears associated with moving. Ruthie's initial response was to justify the move. Then she was able to identify the fears—fear of people, fear of looking foolish and wondering whether she is ready for the move. The more she talked, the more we were able to distinguish the real fear which is that Ruthie doesn't trust herself, thus doesn't trust her decisions.

Using a formula that has worked for me for years, I suggested she was powerless over people and that her thoughts were spinning out of control, thus causing far more fear than is reasonable. (You know that acronym of fear: false evidence appearing real = fear.)

So the cause of confusion was not the decision Ruthie had made to move; it was the false evidence appearing real—fear and not trusting herself. Eleanor Roosevelt said, *"You gain strength, courage and confidence by every experience in which you really stop to look fear in the face."* I asked Ruthie to look each of the identified fears in the face, to welcome and embrace them, then let go and ask Spirit for inspiration and guidance. As she met each fear head on and invited Spirit into the experience, her voice relaxed, the tension diminished and she began to laugh.

We then discussed the option of changing her mind about moving to California. Just because the truck had new tires, the California apartment deposit had been sent, the friend had come to help move—none of that mattered if the move was less desirable than staying in Texas. Even the going away party could be changed to a staying party. She identified her fears and looked them in the face. Her self-confidence grew, her fear lessened and she experienced letting go and asking for Divine Intervention as she inched her way toward her heart's desire—to move to California.

Heart's Desires

THIS PHRASE, *heart's desires,* implies so much. It implies I know what I desire emotionally, physically and spiritually. Quite frankly, I had never paid attention to my heart's desires until I began studying the great metaphysical teacher, Emmet Fox. Fox says that the way to our heart's desire is three fold in nature: *unselfish in motive, forgiveness of others and ourselves, and a general attitude of peace and good will toward all.* This true sense of harmony and freedom permits unobstructed flowing of the Divine Mind through us.

My heart's desires will flow and I will be in the realm of Spirit living a life of prosperity, abundance, joy, peace, harmony, light and love. Is that true? All I have to do is be unselfish, forgiving and have a general attitude of peace and good will toward all and my heart's desires will unfold?

Well, if that's all I have to do, then I am game. I can be unselfish and forgiving. I can act peaceful and have goodwill in my heart for all. Or can I? Can I really be unselfish all day, every day? Can I forgive my first husband for his infidelity? Can I forgive the woman my father married, after my mother died, who literally stole his five children's inheritance? Can I forgive the wretch I worked with who attempted to steal my identity? Can I forgive the man who lied to me about his love for me and his promise to marry, only to be caught in the act of pleasure with another woman?

Am I supposed to have a general attitude of peace and goodwill for these mean-spirited folks and *voilà*— my heart's desires will appear? According to Fox, that is what is required: *unselfish motives, forgiveness, peace and goodwill toward all.*

If that is true, then I need more than just the promise of revelation of these desires—I need proof. I am human and selfish. I am unforgiving and proclaim peace and goodwill but want those who have erred to be punished.

You can see my dilemma—I desire to know my heart's desires and I desire to know that people who have hurt me will be punished. How can these two attitudes meet in the middle of Spiritual Laws? According to Fox, they cannot. Would I rather know and realize my heart's desires? Or would I rather know and realize that those who have gone unpunished are punished?

Today, I would rather know my heart's desires. I've been praying for Spirit to remove unselfish and dishonest motives, for forgiveness of those humans who had hurt me, real or imagined, and for peace and feelings of goodwill for all. I don't have to know if or how those folks who were unkind and hurtful are punished. That is not my business. Fox says my heart's desire comes from Spirit and will be fulfilled by Spirit.

It has been my heart's desire to write and publish

a book for at least ten years. In 2003, I began to write but didn't have the discipline or the full-on desire to write every day. Not until August of 2010 did I sit down and write with purpose, inspiration, direction and yes, desire. Once I committed to the desire of writing the book, took action and shared my desire, then much of what I required has come to me: time, creative ideas, inspiration, direction and offers of assistance with the book's publishing.

Three people offered to assist me with this book within seven days of each other. Two are in advertising and marketing and the third owns a publishing company. Is this proof enough for me? It is today, and I believe more inspired proof is on its way.

What are your heart's desires? Not sure? Well, grab a piece of paper and write them down. Watch what happens in your mind and body. What comes up for you—excuses why these desires cannot be fulfilled? Or action ideas? How many of these excuses involve a selfish thought, a justified anger toward someone, that "get them first before they get you" mentality?

Practice Fox's formula for realizing your heart's desires and then take the initial action toward the heart's desires and watch the Universal Intelligence assist. If I can do it, you can, too.

Where desire doth bear the sway,
The heart must rule, the head obey.
Francis Davison

I want to know how your heart's desires have been fulfilled, so email or comment on my blog what steps you took to begin to receive these desires.
www.judithpepper.com

February

Romance, love, friendship and family

Valentine's Day

DO YOU CELEBRATE Valentine's Day with cards and candy? Do you receive an invitation to a romantic dinner, flowers, hot sex, a poem from a loved one? Or do you dream about being a special someone's Valentine?

I have experienced all the above—celebrating with a special lover, giving and receiving flowers, candy, cards, dinner, hot sex, but never a poem.

One of my favorite Valentine surprises was a dozen tangerine-colored roses on a cold February day when I was living in Taos, New Mexico. I was dating a man who lived 55 miles on the other side of Taos Mountain, and he hadn't mentioned Valentine's Day, much less celebrating together.

I managed a nonprofit agency in Taos and on Valentine's Day, 2001 I was sitting in my office when Cathy, the receptionist, came breathlessly in and asked me to come to the lobby. Much to my surprise and delight the most gorgeous tangerine-colored roses were on the receptionist's desk with a note saying, *"Happy Valentine's Day, Sunshine. xxoo Jim."* For that moment I knew I was cherished and adored by this man. Yes, that Valentine's

Day was spectacular.

Fast forward six years. I had left Taos and returned to Amarillo, Texas and was dating a man who lived in a neighboring state. We had spent the weekend together before Valentine's Day and I mentioned I would like to spend Valentine's Day with him. As I was not working at the time, I would drive the three hours for dinner.

Not only was he not interested in spending Valentine's Day with me, he told me he had plans with his daughters. I did not feel cherished or adored. If only I had not been in denial of his lack of attention, I could have saved myself loads of pain. That Valentine's Day was very troubling and sad for me.

My father's birthday was on February 14th. Oftentimes I could find a card that had both "Happy Birthday" and "Happy Valentine's Day" wishes for him. When I was younger I would buy him candy, a tie, or some such gift. On a few occasions I sent flowers. I loved celebrating his Valentine's birthday with him.

Do you remember the Valentine's boxes we made in elementary school that either sat on our desk or along the counters under the windows? Our names were proudly written on the decorated boxes, and each child was to place a card in each box. That was to teach us care and concern for all the students. I worried on those days whether "he" would give me a special card. Just the thought of writing his name on the envelope and signing my name on the back of the card made my heart palpitate and palms sweat. He never knew my true intentions.

Present day. I've read all the tips on celebrating

Valentine's Day

Valentine's Day as a single woman. All I can say is, "Yuck." Do I really want to send myself flowers? Buy a piece of jewelry as my own lover? Gift myself with a day at the spa? None of that takes the place of a lover putting his arms around me and pressing really close with his lips on my ear, whispering "Be mine." Just writing that made my heart palpitate. My hands got sweaty, just as they did in the second grade before I dropped the card in "his" Valentine card box.

However you choose to spend Valentine's Day—with your loved one, alone, in a candy store, enjoying a day at the spa, being room mother with cupcakes at your child's school—it's a lot like Christmas. There is so much commercial hype that it has lost much of its luster and lust. If a man doesn't spend $100-200 on a dozen roses, $10.00 on a special card, $200.00 on dinner, then he has not shown his undying love for his woman. Not to mention what she does for him.

Now that my father is dead and I have no lover in my life, at this writing, I am going to spend Valentine's Day just like any other day. I'll have a bit of angst about my father's passing, a shallow thought of jealousy for my girlfriends whose significant others, lovers or spouses, will shower them with gifts. Then I will pop out of bed and dance to the kitchen for my first cup of strong, bold coffee!

Friends

"It's the friends you can call up at 4 A.M. that matter."
                              Marlene Dietrich

*I*REQUIRE FRIENDS IN MY LIFE. A few of my friends give me a sense of pleasure and connection with my higher self. A few make me laugh, several make me cry, and one has loved me no matter what. I have always had friends, and that may be due to being the youngest of five children. My brother and sisters were busy living their lives and didn't want me running after them, so I was left to my own devices for companionship.

The longest friendship I have is with Dorla who is my dearest friend. We met in 1972 when I moved to Houston, Texas, and our friendship has flourished and grown over 40 years. We were working for the same Texas agency and both of us needed a friend. I had just moved to Houston, and she was in the middle of a divorce. I needed a friend and she needed a babysitter for her three adorable children during her out-of-town business trips.

Our friendship has withstood marriages, divorces, deaths, moves and even hurricanes. Dorla has seen me at my best and my worst. She has never stopped loving me. We have laughed and cried together. Dorla is the same woman I met all those years ago; she has never altered her values, her personality, and her integrity in these 40

Friends

years, no matter her life circumstances. She did alter her nose, but that is her story to tell.

I recently visited her in Houston and we laughed through Neiman Marcus, created a stir of pleasure in Ulta, and she bought me a Chanel watch for my birthday. We are friends of the mind.

"She is a friend of mind. She gather me, man. The pieces I am, she gather them and give them back to me in all the right order. It's good, you know, when you got a woman who is a friend of your mind."
Toni Morrison

I have male friends whom I adore and trust. Dan, who lives in San Francisco with his partner, makes me laugh with gusto. Sometimes I call him just for the laughter. We have journeyed through recovery work together and I count on Dan to remind me of the spiritual principles that guide me to my highest good. Recently Dan reminded me to embrace my fear and self doubt with, "Hello old friends, I see you are back again." If you don't have a friend like Dan, get one.

I've noticed as I get older that I don't need as many friends. Do you suppose I've become my own friend? I like my own company or perhaps don't need as many diversions as I once did. Many friends have come and gone. Some I miss; others I don't. About some I wonder, whose personality have they taken on today? I have learned not to trust friends whose colors change according to the whim of others. I value women and men who live by integrity and dignity.

Friends are like rainbows—during the rainstorm they appear with big wide smiles of brilliant colors.

"Piglet sidled up to Pooh from behind. 'Pooh!' he whispered. 'Yes, Piglet?' 'Nothing,' said Piglet, taking Pooh's paw. 'I just wanted to be sure of you.' "*

A. A. Milne

---

* Milne, A.A. *Winnie-the-Pooh*. Puffin Books. London: 2005.

I Love You

THERE IS A MAN I HAVE LOVED for twenty years, and I have never told him. It began with lust and a quick tryst resulting in fear and trepidation for both of us. He ran, I hid, the lust died, and love blossomed as I grew to know him as a man rather than the object of my obsession.

Paulo Coelho writes in *The Fifth Mountain* of the love of a woman for the prophet, Elijah: *"She could love him, even if he never knew; she did not need his permission to miss him, to think of him every moment of the day, to await him for the evening meal. This was freedom: to feel what the heart desired…"**

This image of a woman's heart's desire being free as she loved this man without his permission is so powerful. Love liberates and love without possession is the highest form of love, as there are no contingencies.

My love for this man of twenty years has not stopped me from loving other men. In fact, my love for him has propelled me to love other men because the emotion of love is one that I cannot live without. I desire to love and be loved. I desire the passion and pleasure that is only

---

* Coelho, Paulo. The Fifth Mountain. Harper Perennial. New York: 2009.

derived from love. It is like breathing air; I must have it to live and flourish as a woman. The love for the other men has not diminished my love for this man. My love has grown and is a source of joy for me. I love him without possession.

Close your eyes and think of the person you love from a distance—loving him or her as your heart's desire rather than the object of your obsession. Can you feel your heart expand, your world grow larger and your soul take flight? Love liberates our Spirit as we imagine the beauty and magnificence of our love. We are better people for having loved without possession.

Sometimes I imagine telling this man of my love for him. Occasionally when I see him and we greet each other, I think about telling him of my love and wonder what he would say. Maybe I will tell him the next time I see him; maybe not.

My Bold Family

BOLD DEFINES MY FAMILY. My father Joe was the youngest of six boys born to an affluent Baltimore family. My mother, Irene, was one of five children born to an Arkansas farming family. They met in California after my father had joined the Marine Corps and my mother's family had moved there in search of a better life. Joe and Irene had five children, and I was the youngest—the baby of the family.

My grandmother, Lillie Turner Moore, was an entrepreneur. Grandma and Grandpa Moore owned a farm in Oklahoma; they grew cotton, wheat and garden vegetables, and raised chickens. Grandma believed in God, family and hard work. She was a Protestant and practiced her religious beliefs systematically and faithfully. Whatever she put her mind to, she accomplished. Lillie was a master gardener and canned her own vegetables; she was a master seamstress, and she instilled the importance of an education in her five children.

I come from good stock and family traditions of love and caring for your own. Irene, my mother, and Pauline, her sister, graduated from college, as did their husbands and their children. Both of these women taught school,

The Age of Sage

reared their children, created beautiful homes and were honest and trustworthy. One thing stands out—they both had an attitude of happiness.

The following statements are from my sister Joan, her daughter Camily and my cousin Angela. You will quickly see how happiness is a central theme in our family:

Joan Michelle McQuay Hodge, my sister, MSN, Texas, age 65:

"I believe the most powerful physical and psychic energy is to move toward the positive, in whatever area presents itself... be it people, action, or emotion. To consciously and deliberately make the choice to immerse oneself in creating good, and in so doing, developing a pattern of positive response, seems to me to be supremely useful in navigating the waters of life."

Camily Michelle Hodge Teed, my niece and daughter of Joan, MED, Texas, age 38:

"I have the power to choose to be happy. It doesn't matter what I'm doing, it's all in my attitude. I can choose to hate doing the mundane chores, or I can turn on some music and dance the chores away. Life is too short to be unhappy."

Angela Kay Teague Lamb, my cousin, M.S., Texas, age 67:

"For me, each day is a lifetime. It has a beginning which I celebrate, a middle that I live fully and completely, and a satisfactory end. As with life, a day may contain a few small flaws, but taken as a whole, it is filled with wonder and joy. How do I do this? I just open myself to the possibilities that are offered up every day. As for

sadness, you either adapt or expire. I have learned from each and every experience, and decided I wanted to adapt happily and never expire. It is really up to the person to gather up all these experiences, mix them up like a cake batter, and create a beautiful, complete life. I will not deny that there were times I failed to carry out my beautiful plans, but I know that I tried to do my best each and every day."

March

Inspiring actions

I'm Not Inspired Today

WHEN I WAKE UP, WHY am I some days inspired and some days I am not? Where does inspiration come from? Is it a sense of well being? A gift from Spirit? Or is it just a good idea transformed by action and originality? Whatever it is, I am not inspired today.

As I write this I am listening to the soundtrack from the movie, *Eat, Pray, Love.* My favorite song on this CD is "Harvest Moon" sung by Neil Young. I am inspired to sway and imagine being in the arms of my lover as we dance around the dance floor at the Sagebrush Inn in Taos, New Mexico. Oh, I am inspired now.

I am dancing with the memory of Jim, a most passionate lover. I met him in October of 2000 when I was living in Taos, NM and went two-steppin' every weekend at the Sagebrush Inn. I watched him dance and was drawn to him like a magnet—I introduced myself and we began to dance. I am a dancer and dancing with another dancer is like wearing the perfect jeans—they just fit. Jim and I fit.

Jim twirled me around the dance floor and because I had on a short skirt, I was inhibited. I had to run home and put on my jeans so I could dance with him without fear of revealing more than I dared.

What came from that night of dancing was the most extraordinary relationship. Jim was sexy, dangerous, passionate and the best man I have ever had the pleasure to dance with. We parted that night and three weeks later, he returned to the Sagebrush on a Saturday night. He grabbed me and we danced all night long. We went for coffee afterwards and he invited me to his home on Sunday for a pork roast. Darlings, dancing leads to just more than pork roast, but we did eat beforehand.

Jim and I laughed, made extraordinary love, and danced all over Northern New Mexico. The memory of Jim reflects the inspiration I am feeling. He sent me roses on Valentine's Day, he called most every night, we danced every weekend, laughed, cried and made love. We went to movies, cooked meals together and simply enjoyed each other for a year.

This walk down memory lane with Jim has inspired me to write today, as inspiration comes from many things. Music, memories, happiness, sorrow, reflection, joy—put on your favorite music, feel the music and watch what comes up to inspire you to action. It may just be the very thing you heart desired.

Blahsville

I DETEST HAPPY-GO-LUCKY people whose lives appear to be successful in every area. Their hair is always perfect, they wear the newest fashions, they never ever have to try on five different skirts and decide on pants instead. They don't have to wear make up. Who are these women?

Can you tell from the above paragraph, I have the blahs? I feel like a failure today—so what that I chose to quit a job without another in sight, ditch that unfaithful boyfriend and return to Amarillo, Texas five years ago because I didn't know where else to go? So what? So what if I decided to write this book and apply for Good Morning America's Advice Guru, and am waiting impatiently? I feel like a failure.

Do I really think Good Morning America even knows where Amarillo, Texas is? Does GMA want a sexy, gorgeous, intelligent grey-haired 63-year-old woman to give advice? Well, whether I am chosen or not, I am the best applicant they could possibly choose. So come on, call me and give me the job.

I gotta do something. It is too windy to walk, I haven't renewed my gym membership and my phone hasn't rung in days. I have not one man, good or bad, in my life. The man my psychic assured me would appear in October 2010 has not stepped out of the cosmos.

BTW—I hate my hair. I've lost 17 pounds and nothing in my closet fits me. I've taken three pairs of pants to be altered. I am craving a new fall wardrobe and dare not spend my savings on clothes, 'cause I gotta pay the mortgage. I am lonely and horny and since I don't have indiscriminate sex anymore, then sex is all about self pleasure.

Blahs, I got the blahs. So what shall I do with these predominantly self-incriminating blahs? Embrace them. Soothe my soul with a walk in the cold, windy weather, keep writing, eat, drink, or just go on.

I want to go to work and, as Nanci Griffith sings, *"jump off the bus and run into the Woolworth store and buy unnecessary plastic items."* The job at GMA would be such fun for me and different from any job I have ever had.

That's another reason for the blahs. I'm not having fun. When I told a group of my friends in Amarillo that I had applied for GMA's Advice Guru, one laughed. The man who laughed lives a dreary existence and never does the unexpected.

I am feeling better, having written that the creep guy laughed at my dream. Did he do that because he dared not let his own heart's desire out into the light of day? My dream to be GMA Advice Guru is worthy. If my name is called as the Good Morning America Advice Guru, I won't thumb my nose at him and say "ha ha." I will climb aboard the limo and wave goodbye with grace and poise.

The blahs are lifting. The sense of doom and the "what to do next" thoughts are leaving my head. I am going to take a shower, head out the door for some much needed community and go by the gym and renew my membership. The forecast for the weather is warmer afternoon temps, so I can do my regular afternoon walk outside and realize the value of living in a great neighborhood.

Do you have the blahs? Take some action that counteracts those nagging thoughts—take a bubble bath, hug your partner, child or pet, apply your favorite lipstick and flash a smile at the person in the car next to you. Send an email to your friends with your heart's desire and count the reply messages of support.

You are feeling better already because you considered taking one of these actions. The blahs will leave when you leave them alone.

No Safety Net

"Only those who risk going too far can possibly find out how far one can go."

T.S. Elliott

WHEN I SHARED WITH an acquaintance that I had resigned from a job without another job in sight (a safety net), she said "You are a risk taker." Her comment gave me pause to wonder, am I a risk taker? Yes, I take risks. Risks make life worth living for me.

The first risk I remember taking was entering a potato-sack race when I was five years old. The racers step into itchy potato sacks, pull them up to waist level and then hop to the finish line. It was extremely hard and I was awarded a blue ribbon for first place. Why was that so risky? Well, picture a very short and chubby five-year-old girl, hopping in a potato sack against much older and larger children; all odds were against me.

I've taken risks in my life with and without safety nets. My first adult risk was moving to Houston from Amarillo, Texas to work as a caseworker for the Texas Commission for the Blind. This was my first professional job after graduating from college and you may wonder why that was so risky. Picture a 22-year-old woman who had never lived away from her parents, packing her car with a few personal belongings and driving to Corpus

Christi, Texas for a month's training, before going to Houston for the job.

I had never driven alone any further south than Lubbock, which is 120 miles from Amarillo. Corpus Christi is 575 miles from Amarillo and without one thought of failure, away I drove. From Corpus Christi I went to Houston and found an apartment. I was never deterred from this major move even though I knew no one in Corpus or Houston. I had the name of a friend of my sister, and "Beth" took me under her wing, introduced me to her friends and even helped me locate my office building near downtown Houston on Fannin Street.

Risks, or perceived risks, come easy for me. I decide what I want to do and go for it. I can only do the norm for so long and I have to scratch the itch that motivates me to make a change. I've been labeled "risky," "compulsive," "thinking out of the box," even "crazy." Call me what you may, I've had experiences that other folks cannot even conjure up, much less live. The people who label me live in fear of losing the safety they perceive is in their lives.

I've learned there is no permanent safety net for any of us. After I moved to Taos, New Mexico—a perceived risk by many—and lived there for ten years, I returned to Amarillo by way of Santa Fe and Albuquerque. Amarillo is a conservative, mostly Republican town, with a low crime rate and below national average unemployment. The perception of safety is misleading, however.

I was hired at the local medical school and thought this would be my last employer before retirement. I had an employment history with the State of Texas and this gave me longevity and retirement benefits, or so I thought.

I worked with a toxic, rude and cruel person. I spent two years and seven months trying to work in this crazy environment, maintain my dignity and integrity, with retirement as the goal. I had much angst over the idea of leaving, but on July 2nd, 2010, after another degrading incident at work, I looked in the mirror and smiled right before I leapt with no safety net in sight. I decided leaving was better than staying; retirement was no longer the goal.

It had felt like the life blood was being choked out of me, very slowly. Was it risky to leave without a job? Was I pushing the envelope too far at age 62 with no retirement benefits in sight? I had just sold one house and bought a townhouse. What was I thinking?

I had to do what T.S. Elliott described in the opening quote—I had to *"go too far to find out how far I would possibly go."* I have no regrets about leaving the job. I began writing this book, planning workshops for women centered around fun and personal growth, and I applied for Good Morning America's Advice Guru. Good grief, none of these would have happened if I hadn't taken the risk of believing in myself rather than remaining in an unsatisfactory and demeaning job.

As the noted Mama Gena says in her book, *Mama Gena's School of Womanly Arts,* *"I have never known anyone who followed their deepest desires with all out enthusiasm and failed. It is almost as if the Universe gives you a leg up, or a helping hand,*

No Safety Net

when you really go for what your heart desires."

Dive into your life feet first. Leap without looking. Practice on little things first and watch the Universe explode with gifts to assist you along the way. Once you remove the perceived safety nets, the world gets so much bigger. The word "no" is nonexistent. The world truly is your oyster or at least you can wear pearls and say you found them at the bottom of the ocean one day when you dove in without a life jacket.

Safety nets not allowed.

Alphabet Spirituality

DOES YOUR MIND TAKE YOU to neighborhoods that are not safe for you to go to alone? Mine does. Recently I was on my morning walk and my mind had wandered into one of those dark and dangerous alleyways. I forget sometimes my reality of no fallback resources, which has been the making of me as an independent woman. I pay my own bills, buy my own houses, maintain my own car, hire roofing contractors—no fallback resources like a trust fund, a financially generous husband or boyfriend. I am on my own. There I was on my walk feeling alone and financially insecure and wondering what the future held.

I forgot my many professional achievements, my personal achievements and most of all, my faith in my Higher Power. As I cannot tolerate but a few moments in those dark and dangerous alleyways, I knew I had to turn around and run quickly back to safety through a new pathway.

I title this new pathway, the Spiritual Alphabet. It is easy and yet so powerful to navigate with this new image produced to dispel the fears and lies and tap into my hidden resources.

Alphabet Spirituality

Alphabet Spirituality is simply starting at "A" and going through the alphabet to "Z" by thinking of words for each letter that feel good. It trains your point of attraction to positive desires rather than negative drama and trauma. I do this when I am driving, walking, standing in line, etc.—whenever I have time and my mind begins to wander into those unsafe neighborhoods.

Alphabet Spirituality
A – appreciate, awesome, actualize
B – beauty, bounty, bodacious
C – create, comfortable, crusty
D – dance, digest, delicious, dainty
E – elegant, emerald, emerge
F – friends, focus, fine, flirt
G – generous, gorgeous, great, girlie
H – honor, history, happy
I – interesting, intense, imagine
J – juicy, justice, joy, jumping, jive
K – kinky, kind, kiss
L – lemons, luscious, lusty, lick
M – magnificent, money, men, most
N – naughty, nice, notice
O – opulent, opal, ostentatious
P – perfect, poignant, prolific, profound
Q – quirky, quaint, quiet, quick
R – reach, rich, ruby, rose, Rome
S – strawberry, St. Thomas, sexy
T – trust, tryst, tipsy, timely
U – ultimate, umbilical, undulate

The Age of Sage

V – victory, vivacious, virgin
W – worthy, wisdom, willful
X – Xanadu, xiphoid, xeric, X-ray
Y – yikes, yes, yippee, yoni
Z – zebra, zany

This is a starter list for you. Make lists of places you want to visit, clothes you want to wear, men's names, sexy things you want with your partner, jobs. You get the idea. Have fun and let the spiritual alphabet create a new pathway of success and excitement away from dangerous neighborhoods.

April

The joy of simplistic living

I Left the Bed Unmade

I LEFT THE BED UNMADE AS I sat down to write this meditation. A myriad of emotions flooded my central nervous system—guilt, fear, panic, resistance, anger and relief. I did not cave. I left the bed unmade. I kept looking over my left shoulder as my office sits off my bedroom and I see the unmade bed.

What does leaving the bed unmade have to do with anything? Well, my past experiences scream loud and clear, "Get the work done first and then play." Making the bed constitutes "work" and play constitutes "frivolous," and in my family of origin "frivolous" constituted "lazy, undisciplined, imperfect, no account" folks.

Leaving the bed unmade is an act of self possession. I possess the rule book. I make and bend the rules. I own my destiny and if I choose to leave the bed unmade for a day or a week, I can.

Isn't that what we each want? To have the freedom to decide for ourselves, to choose what we desire? Leave something undone for a day or two (not forever) and watch the thoughts that march over your soul. Listen without judgment. Let go of the old idea that everything has to be done and done perfectly. Go deeper and observe your breath—are you breathing or eating air? Stop, take several deep breaths, drop your shoulders and feel the tension leave your body.

The feelings resulting from leaving the bed unmade are symptoms of something much deeper. Tune into the feelings, own them, love them and then release them. Leave the bed unmade, the dirty laundry, the clothes at the cleaners, the half-written report, the unmowed lawn—just leave it and write a new rule that fits you.

Try this on for size: *Il dolce far niente* (the sweetness of doing nothing)—an Italian phrase that speaks loud and clear what the Italians have been doing for centuries. *Il dolce far niente.* Leave the bed unmade. Meditate on the sweetness of doing nothing, doing something different and writing new rules.

Simple Living

BE NICE TO THE GROCERY store clerk. Smile at the waitress, no matter how grumpy she is.

Don't believe everything your doctor tells you.

Read at least one book a month and support your public library.

Treat your children with respect and a sense of fun. Ask them their opinion.

Wear funky clothes—walk with more sass in your step.

Save money every month.

Donate money or goods to your favorite charity.

Buy in resale shops, even if you donate the item back to the store. Support a cause.

Polish your shoes.

Imagine a peaceful world and do your part.

Tip at least 20%; the service staff will always remember you.

Be nice.

Rent the movie *Some Like It Hot*.

Laugh every day.

Cry when you want to, and never apologize.

Give a damn.

Pay your monthly expenses on time and write "Thank you" on the check.

Live your dream.

Count your blessings.

Trust Spirit.

Life—Simplistic or Austere?

DO YOU YEARN FOR MORE life and less excess baggage? Have you reached a pinnacle and heard the drum roll only to realize your heart aches for less, not more? I have. I have been married twice, received major awards for my work, seen national treasures, shaken hands with celebrities, traveled extensively, lived lavishly, only to reach a pinnacle in life to choose simplicity.

Simple living is not forced or unwanted. It is a choice. It is not living in abject poverty or in a communal way. Thoreau defined it: *"Voluntary simplicity as a manner of living that is outwardly more simple and inwardly more rich, a way of being in which our most authentic and 'alive-self' is brought into direct and conscious contact with living."*

I had lived in a large, elegant home with multiple rooms—living room, den, kitchen, breakfast room, dining room, powder room, master bedroom, guest rooms, office, guest bathrooms, patios, three-car garage, storage shed and, believe it or not, there was only me and my husband living in this house. No one but the two of us in the home of our dreams. Nothing wrong with the dreams of youth reflecting prosperity and abundance, but it was the American dream both my husband and I had heard about growing up in Texas.

I had measured my internal value based on external possessions. I had gauged my self-value and worth based on my zip code, area code, fashion labels, home décor, etc. I had maintained ostentatious living to outsource my self-worth. I had allowed greed, pride, ego and external distractions to be my guiding force and yearned for more. Yearning for more became my greatest teacher—each time more was realized, I felt less—less secure, less keen, less poised, less impressed.

I awoke one day and began to ask "When is enough, enough?" How many bedrooms and bathrooms do I need? How many sets of dishes can I use at one time? Do I really need a three-car garage for one car? I counted 35 different (and some the same) black slacks in my closet. I had sheets and towels that hadn't been used in at least two years. Good grief, what had I done? What had I become?

Between 1994 and 2005 I lived in Taos, New Mexico and my home was 900 square feet, with small rooms, large windows and a courtyard that was my outdoor sitting room. When I bought my home, a friend declared, "You could do better." Good grief, how much better could I do? Everything I desired and required was in that precious home.

I simplified my lifestyle and my work to benefit others in Northern New Mexico. I worked with brilliant minds that designed and built public access to, education about and services for the Internet in the remote rural and

Life—Simplistic or Austere?

mountainous region of Taos and the Enchanted Circle. I won a national award for innovative leadership from America Online. I was happier than I had ever been—living simply and being of service to others.

How do you regard your lifestyle today? Do you feel rewarded by who you are or what you have? Do you desire more internally and less externally? I suggest the following inventory to take into account what is motivating you today. It is a guideline to reduce consumption and increase service. Use it for your highest good and for a conversion from more to simple.

Inventory

First, how many people live in your home? Calculate the physical, emotional and spiritual needs of each person. Are these needs being met easily? Extravagantly? Simply? Does your income meet these needs? Are you living within your means or excessively, with credit cards and in debt? Which feels more authentic?

Now, just a simple inventory:

How many coats are in your closet? Have you worn each of them this year?

How many pairs of shoes, boots, tennis shoes, house shoes and sandals are in your closet?

Do you use every item in your garage? Are there seasonal items that are used accordingly? Are there boxes of "stuff" you move around to get to other items? Could the stuff be discarded?

How many phones do you have? How many television sets are in your home? Do you have land lines, cable,

The Age of Sage

wireless that could be shared?

What is your favorite room in your house? Do you have other rooms that are rarely used? Do you need them or just have them?

Is your success measured by your income, the size of the house you own, the car you drive, the schools your children attend, where you vacation? Is your success measured by the amount you give to charity, either in terms of your time or financial resources?

This has been a great exercise for me. I returned to Texas after 11 years in Taos, New Mexico and lost sight of simple living. I vow again to adhere to simple living—to own a smaller home, acquire less by giving away what I don't use, consume less, and be of service to others.

Simple living is a state of mind. Each of us should define simple and appreciate those boundaries. Simply stated, do you have what you need and need what you have? Do you have what you want and want what you have? If so, enjoy your simplistic life style. If not, be open to consuming less and sharing what you don't need. Let go and simply live with what you have!

Thank-you Cards

"Let us be grateful to people who make us happy; they are the charming gardeners who make our souls blossom."
                                        Marcel Proust

GIFTS COME IN DIFFERENT sized packages and with the Internet providing the online avenue to order anything anywhere, any time and for any occasion, we often don't "see" the giver to personally say "Thank you." The information age has rendered thank-you note-writing as superfluous and gift giving has become impersonal. This is why it is even more necessary to personally hand write a thank-you note.

Gift givers like to be acknowledged and appreciated for their effort and the money they had spent on choosing the perfect gift. Have you forgotten how to write a thank-you note? Even if you think it is cheesy, try this simple recipe, and at the end of this narrative, I'll share with you why sending that thank-you note is so important.

Recipe for Thank-you Notes:

✎ Send it no later than seven days after receiving the gift.

✎ Keep a stash of thank-you note cards in your work and home office desk.

✎ Write a short, sweet and genuine message: *"Dear So & So, Thank you for the beautiful scarf and earmuffs. They are perfect for my late afternoon walks on these cold days. You always give the best gifts. Warm Regards/Love/Sincerely"* and sign your name.

✍ Address the envelope, and if you don't have the address, Google the person's name and address. They are usually quite easy to find.

✍ Put a stamp on the envelope and mail it immediately.

No matter how many times you had told the giver "Thank you," the note card will solidify your gratitude and sincerity. You will definitely be connected to the giver on a more intimate level, and next year's gift (and here is the secret to sending thank-you notes) could be more extravagant and arrive earlier than this year's.

If you have children, teach them the etiquette of writing thank-you notes. In our world, conversations tend to be casual. Texting, Facebook, Twitter, email have taken the place of personal communications. A thank-you note can partly transcend this not-so-perfect change and at least make those gift givers aware that you have taught your children manners.

Buy gorgeous, bright note cards to say thank you and be gracious with your gratitude. The gift giver will be thrilled.

May

*Invitations to enjoy finance,
money and abundance*

The Value of Education

MY MOTHER WAS A YOUNG girl living on the family farm in Arkansas during the Great Depression. Her parents farmed cotton, raised chickens for eggs and food, sent all five of their children to school and church, and taught them the Protestant ethic about work and money. They go together—an honest day's work for an honest day's pay.

My grandmother realized that education was an important prerequisite to getting a good job. In the Depression, that meant a high school education. You can only imagine the sacrifices my grandparents had made for their five children to attend and graduate from high school. Grandma knew that farming was hard work with very little pay, and she wanted her children to realize success. Education was the key to that success.

Not only did my mother and her brothers and sisters graduate from high school, four of them graduated from college and several achieved master's degrees. Each of the children achieved college graduation at different times in their lives. My grandparents had no money to send them to college; they simply instilled in them that the value of education equates a better life.

Both my mother and father graduated from college. Daddy attended college on the G.I. Bill benefits and they scraped together enough money each semester for Mother's tuition. Attending college was not easy. With five children, Daddy worked odd jobs and they staggered classes so that when one of them was at school the other was with the children.

Consequently, my parents instilled a similar value for education in their children. We all attended college, four graduated with bachelor degrees, and two with master's degrees. Most of the grandchildren have graduated from college. I am grateful my parents insisted we attended college and even more grateful for the results!

Prosperity and Abundance

"Expect your every need to be met. Expect the answer to every problem, expect abundance on every level."
                                                    Eileen Caddy

WHAT IMAGE DO YOU HAVE with these two words, *prosperity* and *abundance*? Do you conjure up wealth, riches, peace of mind, opulence, plenty of all you desire? Are the things you imagined to be found in your living space now? Do they feel attainable or just a dream of what you wish for your life?

Prosperity and abundance exist in our present exactly as we define them. If you believe you are living in plenty, you are. If you believe you are living in lack, you are. What we think about grows, and the thought energy we create manifests our reality.

These four bold prosperity and abundance principles magnetize and multiply our financial awareness. As you build them into your financial meditations, observe the universal flow of resources zooming your way.

Demonstrate an Attitude of Gratitude

Give thanks for everything you have, including money. Create a prosperity and abundance gratitude list and use expansive words to describe your immediate situation.

✓ Thank you for the crammed and jammed bank account of $78.13.
✓ Thank you for the money to pay the monthly bills; there is money to spare.
✓ Thank you for my magical purse; it easily attracts money.

I carry a million-dollar-bill in my purse that represents the universal prosperity that I desire to achieve.

Be a Good Steward

My mother was very mindful and respectful of her material possessions. She and my father grew up in the Great Depression, and prosperity and abundance were defined differently for their generation. Mother's steward principles consisted of a weekly house cleaning in which we five children participated by cleaning the bathrooms, dusting the furniture, washing and hanging the laundry outside, sweeping and waxing the hardwood floors. My father's stewardship consisted of mowing the yard weekly, washing the car, sweeping the garage and driveway and any other task my mother assigned to him.

As we children got older we ironed our own clothes, changed the sheets on our beds, cleaned the kitchen after the family dinner and mowed the yard. Attending to our material possessions represents gratitude and thankfulness and creates a thriving space. Neglecting our material possessions signifies lack of respect and creates space for destruction and decay.

Spend Wisely

Be aware of your monthly expenses. What do you spend money on? Do you spend over or under your monthly income? Is shopping a necessity or a social event? Do you shop for pleasure and fun? I have enlisted a personal shopper in the past and learned these good shopping tips: never go without a list, don't buy anything that isn't on the list, buy as much as you can on sale or wait until it goes on sale. I seldom pay full price for anything these days.

Determine a set dollar amount and decide you have to wait 24 hours before making a decision to exceed that amount. For me this amount is $200; for some folks it is $100. Honor your decision and you will be surprised at the amount of money you don't spend. I recently lusted after a pair of high fashion boots that were over $200. I waited 48 hours, and upon returning to the store to try them on I decided they weren't nearly as high fashion as I thought and I didn't buy them.

I am not suggesting that you deprive yourself; I am suggesting spending wisely and responsibly. It is no secret, the Universe rewards righteous behavior.

Share

Share what you have with the people in your life and with those who are less fortunate. Give easily and effortlessly without fear of loss or lack. Again, give responsibly. Over giving is embarrassing for the receiver. Share your time, attention, unused household items, unused clothes and yes, your money. Many people tithe to their places of worship. Share with grace and poise and for fun and for free. The Universe showers blessings on sharers. Be someone who shares and enjoy the sense of connection with prosperity and abundance.

Money Magic

*H*OW DO YOU VIEW MONEY? Is it something to attain, work for or to have just enough of? Are you a *have* or a *have not*? Do you love money? Does money love you? Do you live in prosperity and abundance? Do you live in lack and limitation? Who taught you about money? Are you afraid of money?

These questions probe your beliefs about money and help begin your personal conversation about living in prosperity and abundance, no matter how much money you have or don't have. Write the answers to these questions and notice what happens in your body and your mind—do you constrict in certain parts of your body? Is your stomach tight, does your head ache, are your shoulders and hips tight? What about your thoughts? Do they start and stop? Do you feel agitated and angry? Or do you enjoy answering these questions with fluidity and powerful thoughts? Do you feel gratitude for the money you have and that which is coming your way? Do you know how to increase your revenue, income, prosperity and do so with a sense of poise and grace?

A classic cosmic law of prosperity is to practice

blessing the money you have and the money you owe others while sharing your blessings easily and effortlessly. The blessing vibrations create abundance energy for yourself and others.

"For the love of money is the root of all kinds of evil. And some people, craving money, have wandered from the true faith and pierced themselves with many sorrows." (Timothy 6:10, New International Version).

This well-known statement clearly states that the "love of money," not *money*, is the root of all evil. I read this verse also to apply to the fear of money, resentment and being jealous of those who have money. Any negative thoughts I have around money draws even more negativity and perpetuates the cycle of lack in my life, just as positive thoughts about money perpetuate abundance and divine circulation for each of us.

This is what I call money magic. Bless the money you pay out rather than begrudging spending it. Years ago I reframed the monthly process of "paying my bills" to "blessing my monthly expenses." That reframe changed the way I approached using my money to take care of myself.

Try these Money Magical Tools for three months and investigate the energy you create using these new money concepts:

❖ Write "Thank you" on each check for your monthly expenses.

❖ Bless your employer on pay day.

❖ Establish a monthly savings plan, even if it is $20.00. Do it and bless it.

♣ Share with a charity, a church, with people less fortunate each month and bless your ability to share as well as the amount you share.

♣ Bless the money in your checking account, savings account, retirement account—any account holding your money.

A fun and sassy way to increase your appetite for money magic, romance, prosperity, abundance, health (you choose your appetite muscle) is to place currency of any amount on your bed and have an erotic, sexual experience with yourself and/or partner. I call this *sex magic*. I prefer $100.00 bills—they tickle my fancy.

Bless your money; create positive energy with gratitude, service and sharing. The more we give, the more we receive. Our receipts can bring a sense of goodwill and connection to others. This may initiate a new avenue for money or resources to reach us.

Life Rewards

"I've been thinking lately that life is like jumping off that beautiful cliff, overlooking the sea, phenomenal waves crashing below, stunning sunrises and sunsets in the most comforting never-ending dance thru eternity. Yet here we are, just human. And that jump is scary as hell. At times we feel confident and leap out to fly. Other times we cling desperately to the nearest rock. But as I've lived, I've found there's a rhythm to the leaps, a rhythm not always harmonious, but always, always musical and beautiful. And the leaps always get the best rewards."
Cornelia Marsh

I LOVE THIS QUOTE FROM Cornelia Marsh. I envision a woman standing on a cliff overlooking the sea, deciding if she will leap or just look. Act or think. Both require courage. How many times have you leaped and then looked? Looked and then leaped? Looked and decided leaping was not the best action? Leaped and wished you had looked and not leaped?

Unless leaping is not a death leap, I say take the action and leap. Prosperity and abundance are ripe and ready for those who act boldly. What is the worst thing that can happen? If you quit your job, will you lose your health insurance? Do you need your health insurance for a life-threatening illness? Unless you can't afford the COBRA insurance, I encourage you to rethink leaping.

Leaping may come in the form of baby steps rather than leaping off the cliff. The rewards of baby steps are equally as important as the leap itself. Some women map out the path of the leap, others leap into the flow and let the natural events occur. I am more the leaper than the thinker. Both, however, have offered tremendous rewards.

What do you desire? In other narratives in this book I describe making your desire list and sharing it with your friends who can help you. The other ingredient for that desire list to be fulfilled requires action on your part. Do you desire to own a home? Google real estate in your area and review the type of housing you desire. Attend open house events, talk to a mortgage company and get pre-approved for a loan; call a real estate agent and begin viewing houses. Only by taking action will you find the house of your dreams.

I wanted to lose ten pounds. I joined Weight Watchers, followed its meal plan and lost 17 pounds.

I wanted a new car—I test drove new cars for three months and on December 30th, 2009, I bought a new car and got a tax deduction on my income tax. Woo hoo—I didn't know I would get the deduction! Two rewards—a new car and a tax deduction because I acted.

I wanted to move to a warmer climate from Amarillo and started looking for jobs in South Texas where it snows every ten years and the average daily temperature in the winter is in the 60s. I now live and work in South Texas.

Are you getting the picture of how life rewards us? Yes, by taking action. What do you want? What do you desire? Who do you want to date? What job do you want? Do you believe you can succeed in realizing your dreams? You are the chooser, the action taker, the mover and the shaker. If you believe you will succeed, you will take the necessary actions to realize your dreams.

It takes courage to create a life filled with rewards. It takes action to make it happen.

June

Healthy living

Make Dining Fun

I LOVE TO EAT. SOME OF MY fondest memories of family gatherings are meals prepared by my Grandma Moore with fruit and vegetables from her garden, meat from the smokehouse, chickens from the chicken coop. Grandma Moore would fry chicken, make milk gravy for mashed potatoes with real butter and cream, homemade yeast rolls, fresh green beans, sliced tomatoes, and homemade peach or cherry cobbler. The family members in attendance would vary from five to 25. This meal was Sunday dinner after church, and leftovers were served at "supper."

Fun was had by all. The children sat outside and the adults at the dining room table. Grandma always had plenty of dishes and silverware (no paper and plastic in sight) and real butter on the tables. We were encouraged to have second helpings. Sugar-sweetened ice tea was the drink of choice. We children used green onion stems for straws. Laughter, joy, smiles and lots of "ums, ahs and oos"—the symphony of food sounds came from everyone.

In those days people performed hard labor and few of us had high cholesterol or heart disease. Or, if we did, it was never attributed to diet.

Fast forward to the 21st century. Obesity is an epidemic. Children eat from paper sacks. Vegetables and fruit come from cans. Tomatoes taste like plastic. Paper plates and utensils are the norm.

I propose to re-establish some of the dining rituals from my childhood and make eating fun. Try the following:

- Set the table with dishes and silverware and use tablecloths or placemats.
- Arrange fresh flowers as a centerpiece or fresh fruit and have a dessert.
- Give your children and spouse a job—to pour the drinks, put salt and pepper shakers on the table, slice the bread, serve the dinner, etc.
- Serve food family style in serving dishes.
- Say a prayer of gratitude for the food and the person who prepared the meal.
- Turn off the TV, iPhone, cell phone and any other phone.
- Talk to each other—ask each person to share an event from their day.
- Keep talking after dinner while cleaning the kitchen and filling the dishwasher.
- Smile at each other. Laugh.
- Plan the next meal and start over at the top of this list.

Make Dining Fun

Families who eat dinner together are happier and more engaged. Research shows children are healthier, marriages are stronger and the family unit remains intact. The meal doesn't have to consist of four courses. Children learn dining manners, social skills of listening and talking, and they tend to eat better. Just prepare a meal and have FUN.

Healthy Dining

GROWING UP IN A RURAL family working outdoors and performing hard labor—fried meat and potatoes, white bread and sugar were on the daily menu. Over the years I have educated myself about healthy eating, and here are a few of the ways I have learned to eat well:

🍎 Whole grains, bread and pasta (not whole wheat, but whole grain)

🍎 Five to eight servings of fruit and vegetables daily—fresh or frozen

🍎 Vegetables of high vitamin and low calorie count are spinach, kale, broccoli, cauliflower, cabbage, carrots, beets, sweet potatoes. Beets and sweet potatoes are better cooked; the others can be eaten fresh in salads or as a snack. Beans are high in protein and fiber and can make a complete meal with another vegetable, salad and whole grain bread.

🍎 Fruits that are high in antioxidants, low in fat, and are good sources of fiber are strawberries, blackberries, blueberries, raspberries, apples, oranges, pears, bananas.

🍎 Grill or sauté fresh fish (preferably salmon or white fish), skinless chicken, bison and, if you must, red meat.

- Use olive oil, nut oils and avocado oil for cooking and making vinaigrettes.
- Snacks—I cannot live without snacks and these are my favorites:
  o Light microwave popcorn
  o Triscuits and peanut butter
  o Crunchy fruit and vegetables
  o Low-fat yogurt
  o Green olives stuffed with garlic
  o Baked chips and salsa.

During the holidays I look forward to delicious and oh-so-fattening pecan pie. I have a piece after Thanksgiving dinner and save a piece to have with my morning coffee. It's all about bringing back memories of the smells and tastes from my mother's kitchen in the early morning as she prepared Thanksgiving and Christmas dinners. I refuse to give up the connection to family and the heart-felt love that inspired those family dinners. One or two days a year of pecan pie, mashed potatoes with butter and gravy made with turkey fat will not kill me as I enjoy a walk down memory lane reviewing food of years past.

Eating healthy is fun and takes commitment. I feel better physically, emotionally and spiritually taking care of myself. If you don't already eat well, try two to four weeks of healthy eating as I have described above. You will probably lose a few pounds, feel more energetic and note fewer cravings for high-carbohydrate foods. Are you game?

Better living through better eating.

"Use It or Lose It"

REMEMBER YOUR CHILDHOOD days when riding bikes, roller-skating and playing outside until dark was the norm? My brother and sister and I used to go to a neighborhood park every day in the summer. We rode our bikes or walked the block and met up with our friends. Sometimes our mother would bring us lunch to the park, sometimes we went home, but the point is, we were always doing something outside.

The public schools required gym classes as part of the curriculum and even though I thought they were boring and dull, I moved my body. College gym classes offered modern dance, tennis, golf and even bowling. I loved modern dance and excelled, as it involved creative movements rather than rote exercises.

Okay, so what's my point? You gotta get up and get moving. The merits of physical exercise are hard to ignore. The Mayo Clinic endorses seven benefits of exercise. According to them, exercise:

1. improves your mood
2. combats chronic diseases
3. helps manage your weight
4. boosts your energy level

"Use It or Lose It"

5. promotes better sleep
6. puts a sparkle in your sex life
7. it can be FUN.

Only three out of ten Americans exercise regularly. If you are not one of the three, then join the ranks with a simple start. You can join a gym and even hire a personal trainer. If you aren't a joiner, then invite a friend to begin walking 30 minutes a day, four to five days a week. Or begin walking alone. Walking alone for me is a form of meditation and a quiet time when I can focus on myself and digest the day's events.

Join a gym, join a yoga or Pilates class, enroll in ballroom dancing or Zumba classes. Any activity is better than none.

My exercise regime consists of a two or three-mile walk in my neighborhood four to five times a week, weather permitting. If not, I go to the gym. I use eight and ten pound weights, and while watching the news or evening television programs I do repetitive exercises to strengthen my upper body and arms. I do 50 squats and 20 pushups.

The result of weight training is toned arms and back, gorgeous shoulders and a firm stomach. I've been told I look great in sleeveless tops and my LBD (little black dress). My butt is firm and I still wear bikinis at the beach. I hope this is incentive enough for you to get up and get moving. The life you save will be your own.

What's Your Pleasure?

*Pleasure: "enjoyment or satisfaction derived from
what is to one's liking."*
Webster's Dictionary

HOW DO YOU DEFINE PLEASURE? What do you conjure in your mind with the word? Sensual in nature? Happiness? Sinful? Hedonistic? Joyful? Doing what you like? Self indulgence?

Each of us daydream about what would make us happy or give us pleasure. A few of us seek and find it. Some of us deprive ourselves of pleasure fearing it will burn the very soul from our being.

Please indulge me while I make a case for your pleasure.

Pleasure and fulfilled desires are food for the soul and our mental health. Regena Thomashauer, founder of the School of Womanly Arts in New York City, teaches "self-indulgence is the key to self-empowerment." Regena teaches women to identify their desires and dreams that define their happiness. I took three of her classes and was transformed into a Sister Goddess, a title given to women who graduate from her classes. I learned how to identify what I desire, what would give me pleasure and to take the necessary actions to please myself.

Are you feeling full or empty? Deprived or indulged? What do you like to do? What gives you pleasure? When

What's Your Pleasure?

did you do it last? What are you feeling toward your family, husband, boyfriend, children, work, employees, employer, friends and, most importantly, yourself? Are you finding pleasure simply in the act of doing, or are you waiting for an *attagirl* from that list of people?

Are you familiar with the proverb, "If momma ain't happy, ain't nobody happy?" Let's reframe that to "If momma's happy, everybody is happy." Abraham Lincoln said, *"Most folks are as happy as they make up their minds to be."*

Pleasure, happiness, joy, delight, bliss equate to doing what one likes to do. Living a happy life requires taking responsibility for our own happiness. I like to make a pleasure list of what is easily attainable and obvious and then add those desires and dreams that some may call a bucket list. For our use, let's call this a pleasure list.

Get your journal and write at the top of the page, "Pleasure List." A few examples that come to my mind that are attainable and obvious are a turkey and avocado sandwich at my favorite health food store, a skinny vanilla latte at Starbucks, a phone call to my sister, flowers for my home, a bubble bath with candles (phones turned off and no interruption), reading a novel or magazine, a mighty gym workout, sex with my lover, preparing a favorite recipe. Okay, now you write an attainable list of your favorite pleasure items.

Notice your mind and body relaxing just by writing the list. Commit daily to savoring at least one simple pleasure from your list. Check each item off as it is accomplished and add new ones. Pleasure is in the eye of the beholder, and it is up to each of us to make it happen. Make simple pleasures a priority. The results will astound you.

Write another list that might seem unattainable and obscure. Write that list with as much ease and poise as you wrote the attainable list. Examples that I have written and have consequently been brought into my reality are international first class travel, a man who has eyes only for me, a hot stone massage at no cost to me, a townhouse, and oh, so many more.

In 2008 I wrote a bold list of desires and included was a fabulous gift for my 60th birthday. In May 2008 my friend Jennifer invited me for an all-expenses-paid trip to Majorca, Spain to spend my 60th birthday on her lover's private yacht. Not only did she invite me, she also invited our friend Melanie. Melanie and I met in Atlanta where she and I received complimentary first class travel to and from Spain from her longtime friend who works for Delta. Jennifer and her lover met us at the airport on the island of Majorca. We spent four nights on the yacht off the coast of Ibiza—sunning, eating, dancing in the moonlight and lolling in luxury. And there is more…

After the fabulous yacht experience, Melanie and I spent two nights alone in Majorca. We visited the Cathedral of Santa Maria of Palma, built in 1229, and took pleasure in the sights and sounds of this gorgeous seaside city. At dinner we met two Swiss bankers and they fell madly in lust with us. All our expenses were paid again except for our hotel room. Meals, cabs, drinks, all were paid by Rudy and Werner. They hosted our visit to the Miro Museum, lunch and dinner in fabulous *al fresco* restaurants and after-dinner drinks at Abaco Bar. These men wanted only to serve us and enjoy our company.

Pleasure in such magnitude I could not imagine, and only because I wrote my BOLD pleasure list and then let go of how and when the Universe would fulfill my dreams.

I have also experienced being with a man whose eyes were only for me (a story for another time!). I live in a gorgeous home. I am treated regularly with complimentary massages. I've learned to accept invitations that seem obscure and let the events flow easily and effortlessly as my desires come to fruition.

Get busy; write both lists—the obvious and the obscure. Hold nothing back. Be bold and enjoy the results of paying attention to your mind, body and soul. Pleasure creates a sense of connection to the Universe. The benefit of enjoying our pleasure is seen in the glow of our skin, smile on our faces, lilt in our voice and bounce in our steps. Please yourself as often as necessary. Healthy living requires it.

July

Success

Mistakes Are Spirit in Action

*E*ASY TO SAY AND READ, HARD to put into practice.

Most recently, you will remember, what I called a mistake was a job with a Texas agency and having to deal with the silly, immature and mean youngster who was my boss. Three years ago I wrote down my desires and that I did not want to be the boss again, having been "the boss" for over 25 years. The Universe listened carefully and *voilá*, a mid-management job appeared and I accepted it. Good grief, Charlie Brown, what was I thinking?

I spent several years working in that job which was totally unsatisfying for me personally and professionally. When I realized the dissatisfaction I felt—the dread of getting out of bed, getting dressed and driving to the job—was not a mistake, I did what any sane woman would do—I resigned from that dead end job.

How many life challenges have we called mistakes? Marriages, divorces, relocations, purchases, children, lovers, excursions, the list is ad infinitum. It is only in retrospect that we can learn to see these "mistakes" as learning experiences that help us grow and blossom within the Universe. Not one successful person I know has lived a life of ease and perfection, including myself.

I believe I create my own reality, just as I did when I stated loud and clear, "I don't want to be the boss anymore." *Voilá*, the reality of working at the dissatisfying job. Two years, seven months and five days later, I yelled loudly and profoundly, "Okay, I get it, I am a boss. Bring on the executive job."

What have you created in your reality that you are calling a mistake? What do you need to reframe, adjust and recreate? Emmet Fox, the metaphysical teacher, suggests, *"Any seeming evil, any mistake made by you or someone else is only a false belief (often terribly real in appearance, but still a false belief)—a kind of dream. All there is of it is the belief in your thought and that of certain other people."*

Freedom

WHAT DOES FREEDOM mean to you? Freedom for me means, as Janis Joplin sang, *"I have nothing left to lose."* When self-will has drifted me off the spiritual course and I am being tossed about in the ocean of life like a tiny matchbox, I have nothing left to lose. I am not even afraid. I am lost. The freedom that comes from the loss of spiritual connection is the freedom that pulls me back to shore. I find myself on my belly surrendering to Spirit, asking for freedom from self-will.

Spiritual freedom is the serenity and peace that surpasses all understanding. It is poise, calm, divine design, faith, joy and rest. It is breathing easily and effortlessly, it is trusting that no matter what, all is well. It is believing that my life has purpose and meaning simply because I am alive. That I was created to live and give meaning to my life by being in the spiritual flow.

Personal freedom for me is being free of fear and you can fill in the blank by defining the reason behind the fear. Freedom from fear is a direct result of the faith I have in Spirit. The more I let go and trust the results of turning my will and life over to Spirit, the more freedom

The Age of Sage

I realize.

Freedoms I cherish:

✌ Living safely and comfortably in the United States of America.

✌ Knowing the rules and having the choice to bend them, break them, or follow them.

✌ Calling any guy I desire and asking him to ask me for a date.

✌ Freedom from addiction.

✌ Inquiring minds—mine and others', exploring life and life's nooks and crannies.

✌ Self-expression in fashion, music, friends, love, sex, joy, Spirit—living my life without boundaries.

✌ Equal opportunity after age 60.

✌ To make serious mistakes and be applauded for the courage of trying.

✌ Stating openly my political beliefs without fear of reproof from employer or friends.

Snippets of freedom from other freedom hunters:

"No underwear." Clarence Lamb, my cousin, Houston.

"Being able to PRAY when and wherever I feel the need to do so." Tina Burks, Amarillo.

"Freedom is the ability to choose and not be enslaved to someone or something." Stephenine Nunn, Amarillo.

"Freedom's just another word for nothing left to lose."
       Kris Kristofferson

Take the Next Right Action

FEELING STUCK AND WITHOUT direction? Unable to accept life on life's terms? Not able to determine the next right action? Not knowing what next action to take reduces many of us to quivering bundles of fear and despair. These feelings may come from a major life challenge or from something as simple as preparing for a presentation at work. Whatever their source, they are real and can emotionally debilitate.

Our job is to tap into the energy of the despair and step out of the darkness and into the light. How does one take that step? How does one mentally observe the darkness rather than wallow in it? And in the observation, how do I step up and out into the light?

My friend, Melanie Erickson, cranial sacral practitioner, has taught me to pay attention to my body when I am feeling fear, despair, sadness—any negative emotion. Becoming acquainted with my body's reactions is necessary for me to construct a prescription for physical release and to step out of the fear and into the light.

A three-pronged prescription:

* Acknowledge the fear, despair, sadness—whatever the emotions are that have dropped you to your knees:

o "Hello, old friend, I see you have returned." Be gracious and generous with your acknowledgement, and welcome these feelings into your bosom.

o Embrace them with love. Many of us have denied these feelings because they represent failure rather than our being human.

* Describe to your old friends the feelings, that you are intentionally releasing them from their place in your heart as they no longer serve a useful purpose.

* Then, take the next right actions:

If you are home:

* Go for a walk outside—let your mind wander in nature.
* Pack up and go to the gym.
* Clean the bathrooms, sweep the garage, vacuum the carpet.
* Bake a cake, dinner rolls, cookies, pie. Do something creative and purposeful to replace the feeling.
* Sew—mend a torn garment; hem those pants that you bought three months ago.
* Do something physical.

If you are at work:

* Get up from your desk and walk through the building.
* Write the letter you have put off since Monday.
* Clean your desk.
* Answer the phone messages.
* Walk outside even if it is 15 degrees outside and

snowing.
   * Do something physical.

Move your body and your mind will follow. Physically taking the next right action literally moves the fearful energy out from your head and body and creates positive energy and space. Notice, when you begin moving, that feelings, even if short-lived, come in the form of hope, self-confidence and yes, even serenity. Also, notice that the challenge that initially caused the fear seems obtainable. That is the goal—to decrease the grip of the fear and take the actions required for success.

You are now ready to develop the PowerPoint presentation that caused you such grief. You can schedule the meeting with the lawyer, discuss your child's absences at school, ask for the raise, etc. Whatever the challenge, you are now prepared for success free from the fear.

How to Thrive at Work

DO YOU WORK OUTSIDE the home? Do you love or hate what you do? Has it become mechanical or is your work creative and fun? Do you earn a great salary or just get by? Are you the boss or the employee? Do you have your dream job or is it a nightmare? Have you become a robot who gets up, gets dressed and goes to work, or do you pop out of bed anticipating the work day?

I have had only two jobs that I define as nightmares and both were with the State of Texas. Both bosses were women and in both I excelled and, quite frankly, would have been a better boss. I learned some great tools while working for these two women, though. Use them as you will.

Thriving at work:
* Smile. Smile at everyone.
* Laugh as if you had a secret—it makes everyone feel like a co-conspirator with you.
* Dress becomingly every day. Wear red even if it isn't your color. Red is a powerful color and it stimulates visually and emotionally.

- Bake (yes, bake) homemade snacks for the office or the office kitchen. It is a personal gift for your co-workers that says you care.
- Arrive early for work and be easily prepared for your day.
- Smile and acknowledge everyone in your office every morning, regardless of what happened the day before. Ask about families, pets, and hobbies—be informed.
- Make friends with the secretaries and facilities manager; they know the layout of the building, the technical infrastructure, and love to help. Every time they assist you, acknowledge their expertise.
- Take pride in the work you are assigned.
- Acknowledge a job well done to both colleagues and supervisors.
- No matter what, keep your emotions at bay. If possible, remove yourself from the person or charged situation to let off steam.
- Respect every person in the workplace, even the nightmare boss.
- Be open to change and learning new techniques and policies.
- Be genuine in your communication and treatment of others.
- Send handwritten thank-you notes to vendors who provide services to your office.
- I am not big on office gift exchanges, but if your office has parties and gift exchanges for holidays and birthdays, participate.

* Keep water cooler gossip at bay. It carries a huge emotional charge if something you say is overheard or misinterpreted.

* Leave early occasionally.

* Schedule your vacation and mental health days.

* Be grateful for the job you have and network for the next job—it could be your dream job.

* Oh, one more thing—have fresh flowers on your desk. Flowers open hearts and can increase creativity among employees.

August

The joy of giving and receiving

Buy the Raffle Ticket

I BOUGHT A $50 RAFFLE TICKET several years ago to support a small community arts agency in Taos. The agency hosts this annual fundraiser and I always have a fleeting thought of winning. I sent my check in, received the raffle ticket in the mail, threw it away and counted my blessings that I can support this agency with my $50.00.

I was quietly minding my own business, watering pots of begonias, petting my cat Flo and looking for my other cat, Dante. When Dante appeared and we three walked inside, I had a message on my answering machine. Imagine my surprise as I heard, "Judith, it's Ron. You are the winner of the grand prize of $1,500 worth of products from the Sleep Sanctuary in Taos." OMG, I won this year! I won. I danced, I cried, I called Ron back to verify this was not a joke. It was not a joke. I had won.

So, you might say, what's the big deal? Here's the BIG deal—I didn't have a job. When I bought the raffle ticket I had resigned, and knew there would be no more monthly paychecks until the next job. I didn't buy the ticket to win; I bought the ticket because I believe

The Age of Sage

in giving. Giving is a joyous thing. It creates a sense of connection with the receiver. I know how to buy a ticket and give, job or no job.

I felt the intensity of Spirit's blessings on me. Did Spirit guide the hand in the jar to pull out the ticket with my name on it? I don't know. My name got drawn because I bought the ticket. I have learned you have to give to receive and you have to receive to give. It's the cycle of giving and receiving; one does not occur without the other.

The more I give, the more I receive; the more I receive, the more I give. I used to sell my clothes in resale shops and have garage sales and make a penny on a dollar. Now I give my clothes and household items to my friends or domestic violence shelters. What I get in return is astounding.

I gave my brother a lawn mower, and he in turn came to my new townhouse and hung my art, curtain rods and full-length mirror. Who do you suppose was on the receiving end? You can bet the lawn mower was not worth his time or effort or knowledge of hanging art and curtain rods. On the other hand, Joe needed a lawn mower. We both gave and received. I still think I came out better.

So pop into your closet, your garage, your attic and yes, even your bank account. Create a stack of clothes, books, pots and pans. Write a check or give of your time and talents. Give and keep on giving, and open your heart to receive. As your hand gives and your heart receives, your world will expand. You might even smile more, and

Buy the Raffle Ticket

quite possibly, you could win $1,500.

Giving is better than getting. Receiving is a result of giving. Or is it giving is a result of receiving? Oh, heck, I am confused. Just do one or the other because you can.

smiling

DORLA HAS BEEN MY BEST friend for 40 years. I met her in 1972 when I had moved to Houston, Texas for my first job after college with the Texas Commission for the Blind. I was 23 and she was 37. She was in the midst of a divorce with three young children and I was on my own in the big city of Houston. Our friendship has grown over these 40 years and most recently we celebrated my 63 birthday at the Mockingbird Bistro in Houston.

Dorla responded to my request to women I admire to write a narrative on living a Bold Life. Below is Dorla's reply:

"Oh Judith, how fantastic. Here are my words and use them as you wish. You know I can't just do 50. Just use any you want for your book and keep the rest for yourself.

"When I go out I wear makeup and nice, chic "me" outfits to suit the occasion. When I stay in I do the same. The most important thing I always wear, truly am never without it, is a great big smile.

"During 77 years of a great life the smile has served me best. A smile given is a smile gotten. Smiles come back to me from all kinds of people. Little bitty babies, very old men and women, even

surly teenagers. People from all walks of life are complimented when you smile at them because it means you have acknowledged them in a personal way. I like to think it makes them feel a little more important—I truly believe it does.

"You can smile in the most public places or the most private ones. Sit in a huge auditorium and catch the eye of the person delivering an important address and smile and nod. Do that every time that speaker's gaze comes close to you. Soon you will notice that the speaker is looking at you more and more and you will see at the dais an ego being inflated.

"Smile at a person on the street who appears to be homeless, with a grocery cart full of worldly possessions, an unwashed body and filthy clothing. The first time the person may be wary and seem unresponsive. Go by again the next day (they are often in the same spot) and smile again—a great big friendly kind of smile. By the third time the person may mumble with a shy grin, 'Szat you?'

"You step into an elevator and one person is there. As soon as you make eye contact put on your best good morning kind of smile, the one with your whole face, your eyes and your heart. In most cases you will get a nod, a smile, or a good morning in return.

"Go boldly into the world with a smile. You are the one delivering the gift."

Thank you Dorla for smiling at me for 40 years.

Receiving

ARE YOU A GRACIOUS RECEIVER? Do you smile and say, "Thank you" when given a compliment, an acknowledgement, a gift? Or do you negate the compliment and try to diminish the giver's thoughts about you? Learning to receive is necessary as we progress personally and spiritually.

I have a good friend who spends the spring in Florida each year. The year of my second divorce she invited me to visit her and spend two weeks lolling in the sun and surf outside her beach house patio. I wanted to go, but with the divorce, money was tight and I didn't have enough for the flight and two weeks of expenses on the beach. My friend offered to pay for the airline ticket and she reminded me that the expenses would be few as we were staying in her home.

My immediate response to her offer was to not accept. How could I let her pay for my airline ticket? That was outside the realm of generosity and I couldn't imagine taking that kind of gift. My friend was very kind and understanding and proposed that in order for me to learn to give, I must learn to receive. She wanted me to be with her and enjoy the beach, heal from the wounds of the divorce and have fun. I decided I would try accepting her gift.

We had an absolutely wonderful time. We laughed, walked the beach, ate great food and I knew I was in the place where I was meant to be at that moment. Ten years later, two of my friends and I were planning our annual trip to Las Vegas and one of my friends said she would have to cancel as she did not have money for the flight. I thought about the gift I had received those ten years before and offered to buy the ticket. Just as I had done, my friend initially refused. But after I shared my own story of learning to receive, she accepted the gift. Needless to say, our Las Vegas trip was so much fun.

Refusing a gift diminishes the giver and the receiver. Genuine givers give unconditionally, and we must learn to receive unconditionally. This next week, notice how you receive. When someone offers to buy your lunch, receive. When the person in front of you holds the door open, receive. When your loved one hugs for no reason, receive. When your boss gives you an acknowledgement for a job well done, receive. Receive each gift with an open heart.

Be prepared to receive and realize the truth in this statement from Johann Wolfgang von Goethe, *"Human life runs its course in the metamorphosis between receiving and giving,"* and from Alex Haley, *"When you clench your fist, no one can put anything in your hand, nor can your hand pick up anything."*

Open your heart, your mind and your hands, and RECEIVE.

Psychic Session

DURING A CHALLENGING TIME in my life I did what very few Texas women do—I consulted a psychic! I hear the laughter now from the few Texas women who have consulted a psychic because they understand the cultural clash.

The psychic suggested I would impact many women through education, writing, speaking and as we pursued these levels of impact, I disclosed my deep desire to write a book. She immediately encouraged me to pursue the book development as it would lead to even greater pursuits of fulfilling my personal goals. She encouraged me to write about my bold life and thus much of this book's content reflects my life challenges, passages and situations.

This book is a direct result of the perfect timing in my life and the encouragement from the Universe through my psychic. There are many channels pointing the way to personal and professional opportunities, if I open my heart and head into the unknown!

To assist me in the transition from a dead end job, I was introduced to Ivette Principe, my psychic, by a good friend. Having never consulted a psychic I was leery. But

Psychic Session

the transition I was considering was very frightening, and since Ivette came highly recommended, I decided to schedule a session.

Our first session lasted one and a half hours. I was amazed at Ivette's immediate grasp of the circumstances, her intuitive and supporting predictions and guidance. She immediately recommended that I quit the job I held. When I told her I had already given my resignation, her exact words were, "Thank God, we won't have to go through that."

Our session followed these strains of conversation and Ivette's insights:

★ I had been working in negativity and with someone whose fear of survival had permeated my consciousness. As I am empathic, I had personalized the fear and made it my own.

★ I was to take the entire month and rest. Quitting the job had slammed on my "breakers" and my system was in shock. My energy was fragmented, stagnant and I was not at my best.

★ The three jobs that had presented themselves were not going to materialize as I was not ready for work.

★ She repeatedly encouraged rest and relaxation.

★ A book was in me—a very important book that I had yearned to write and now was the right time.

★ The book was very timely and I would be writing it in tandem with something else. Again, she recommended taking a break; the energy and resources were coming.

★ I would be involved in a radio show, consulting,

The Age of Sage

working with women, and it would be centered around the book.

★ My higher self was bringing me a compatible match in a man—we will have strong intellectual, emotional, and physical connections. Ivette described his physical characteristics as well as our mutual attraction to each other.

★ I was meant to have this transition. I had been in denial of the lack of fulfillment in my life. I had emotional flu and I required dream time, contemplation time and alone time.

I have since had other sessions with Ivette and here are the predictions that have transpired since taking actions based on her predictions:

★ The book will be edited by an editor in New York City.

★ A radio show with public speaking events is under negotiation.

★ I am developing my business for public speaking, online interactions with women and partnering with other women-focused businesses.

★ I am rested. I am highly energetic, highly impatient and have continued to be in surrender to the pathology and addiction to suffering. This is a process and thanks to Ivette and Melanie Erickson, sacral cranial practitioner, I am healing from the addiction to suffering.

★ I have met men, none of whom interest me, as my energy has been focused on writing this book.

Ivette's insight, intuitive focus and even her business experience have been very helpful, as I have taken action to transition and reinvent myself. When I left the dead end job, I had no idea, nor cared, what I would do next. The series of events that occurred were beyond my wildest dreams. Yes, I took action. Yes, I quit the job. And I called Ivette. Our decision to work together (my trusting her guidance and her trusting my desires) has created an incredible relationship, and my dreams of being self-employed, inspiring women and having fun are coming to fruition.

I opened my heart and mind to receive Ivette's gift of extraordinary, higher-level spiritual states of being. I am thrilled I laid aside the preconceived ideas of working with a psychic.

Should you be interested in seeking a higher consciousness of participation in your life and life desires, I recommend Ivette Principe to assist you on this path. You can learn more about her at: *www.mydirectpsychic.com*.

September

Facing fears and finding the gift

Finding Faith in Fear

*L*ET'S CUT TO THE CHASE. We are all afraid. What are you afraid of today? Which fear is stopping you from claiming what you desire? Fear comes in many forms: worry, anxiety, remorse, depression, addiction, pride, ego, judgment, anger, jealousy. Fear is usually attached to losing something that we have or not getting something that we demand. Fear is an emotion, and an emotion is the body's reaction to the mind. *"As a woman thinketh in her heart, so she is."* James Allen, British spiritual writer.

Elkhart Tolle, spiritual teacher and counselor, writes, *"You can always cope with the present moment, but you cannot cope with something that is only a mind projection—you cannot cope with the future."* So if I am to cope in this life I must learn how to let go of fear, live in the moment and trust there is something to replace the destructive and powerful fear. What is the force bigger than fear? My big force is faith in Spirit.

Surely you have heard or read, "The opposite of fear is faith." If that is true, where does this faith come from and in what do I place my faith? I cannot wish the fear away. If I am to live in the moment, then I have to believe

The Age of Sage

that while in that moment I am safe and protected from the past and the future. And if I am to rely on a Higher Power, God, Goddess, Spirit, Infinite Intelligence, then it makes sense that I have to believe this Infinite Power is bigger than my fear.

Trusting my finite self is a guaranteed failure. In each circumstance in which I have placed my sole trust and faith in myself, I have failed. Failure is my catalyst for seeking a power greater than me. Admitting complete defeat and surrendering to the unknown Power has brought results that my small mind cannot fathom, much less comprehend.

The first step is to admit you have failed and ask Spirit to help you solve your problem. The next step is to let go of the circumstantial fear and pretend that Spirit has an answer. Praying for faith and being still, giving Spirit time to work in your life, without any of your fine assistance, will reap benefits beyond your greatest imagination.

While you are being still and waiting for Spirit to work in your life, try this simple formula to identify and be rid of the fears your ego has been weaving in your mind. Get a sheet of paper and write at the top, "I Am Afraid of" and make a list of your fears. Number each of your fears, and when the fears have all tumbled out and you can't come up with another one, stop writing.

In previous narratives I have written about developing an ally or allies in your Bold Game of Life. One of these allies will be the sounding board for your fear list. Call the ally you trust most and read them your list of fears, leaving nothing out, no matter how embarrassing or revealing. Once you and your ally acknowledge the fears, then together ask your Spirit to remove them and replace the fears with faith and courage.

Go back to your fear list and for each fear, write, "I have faith in…" and replace the fear list with a faith list. For instance, "I am afraid of not having enough money," "I am afraid of being alone," "I am afraid of not finding the perfect job." Your faith list would then read, "I have faith I have enough money," "I have faith in being alone," "I have faith in being hired for the perfect job."

Notice immediately how your faith muscle grows and that you are building a faith foundation in Spirit. You can now enjoy peace of mind, knowing Spirit is doing for you what you cannot do for yourself.

I do not believe women or men can live a fearless life without help from a Power greater than themselves. Finding faith in fear is a direct result of realizing how limited we are in our ability to change our reality based on fear. Faith doesn't totally remove the fear but it does take me out of the equation long enough for me to relinquish my pride and ego and ask for spiritual guidance and help. Faith is the opposite of fear and fear leads me to faith.

What are you afraid of today? Which fear is stopping you from claiming that which is rightfully yours?

Feel free to contact me if you ever need a fear friend; I am available to help you heal your wounds and diminish your fears. Go to *www.judithpepper.com* and send me an email.

Faced My Fear of a Bridge Game

YOU ARE READING THE TITLE and thinking, what does fear have to do with a Bridge game? Well, I received an invitation from Peggy to be a fill-in, a fourth, at one of her longstanding Bridge games, and old familiar fears surfaced as quickly as oil in the oil fields. I honestly began to sweat as I replied, "I haven't played Bridge in 30 years." Peggy said, "No worry, it will all come back to you once you are holding the cards after the first deal." Wouldn't that be easy if the source of the fear was actually playing Bridge? That would be simple.

My fears stemmed from self-esteem issues. This group of women plays Bridge at the Country Club. I always wanted to be a member of the Country Club, but growing up in a middle class family with five children, country club membership and monthly dues were not in my parents' budget. I grew up with the feeling there was something wrong with me and that is why we weren't members of the Country Club. My friends who were members, well, they had nothing wrong with them or their families.

It is a terrible thing for a child to define herself

Faced My Fear of a Bridge Game

around lack and limitation. That definition poured over me like Niagara Falls and was one of the sources of the great divide I lived with for a very long time. I felt I was never good enough for the A team. My young life consisted of being on the B team—never a cheerleader, band twirler, beauty queen, or a football star's girlfriend. Never a Chosen One.

I was a chubby child and teenager. I was very smart, with quick wit, but not beautiful, intimidated by the beauty queens, the "in" crowd and those football players. The pain that streamed from the belief of that kind of lack and limitation helped strengthen the conviction that there was something wrong with me. "Surely, if I were different, all would be well."

I tenderly caress myself and Soul today as I recall what I have done to make myself different. I lied about who I was, the very essence of Spirit's creation, and I lied. I longed to be the same as those beauty queens, cheerleaders and thin girls who were the football players' girlfriends. And when I realized that was never going to be my path I veered off like a drunk bull hauler on a back county Texas road.

I learned how to smoke, drink and screw like a mad woman. If I was going to be number one at something, it was at least going to be something big. Big like a Grand Canyon boulder. And thus my journey of being something began at about age 19. I began to drink with the best of the guys, play Eight Ball Pool and dance. I learned I had a commodity that would buy me a few minutes of "love and admiration." That drove me into the self loathing and hatred that took years to crawl out of and heal.

Simply put, I crawled into the well of alcohol and didn't come out until age 36. I drank alcohol excessively for 21 years. Not every one of the 21 years was all bad, but every one of the 21 years and my choices poured salt and rubbing alcohol on the wounds until I was a walking wounded paralyzed young woman, still believing there was something wrong with me.

On August 25th, 1984, I was surrendered by the disease of alcoholism and since that day have never taken another drink. I attend and celebrate these years of sobriety in a Twelve-Step Program. My gratitude is difficult to articulate to those who have not walked the path of recovery. Just know, I am grateful I live a life of dignity and integrity today.

Through the Twelve-Step Program I found a grace and love that we in those rooms call "the language of the heart." Slowly and with the help of many people, I learned how to love myself and to believe there is everything right with me. I believe today, had my parents been members of the Country Club, those 21 years of alcoholism and self-loathing would still have happened. I would have crawled into the well of drink with or without membership at a country club.

So, do you see why the Bridge game was such a big deal for me? Not only did I face the fear of inadequacy in the very country club that had been the nemesis in my game of life, I faced that precious little girl who so wanted to belong and then eased her in and let her see that she belongs everywhere, no matter what or where

Faced My Fear of a Bridge Game

she is.

I've learned to not apologize to anyone or anything for who I am or from whence I have come. I have learned we all have demons and fears that have stymied us and caused great pain and cruelty. I have learned to embrace the fear and listen to the heartbeat behind the fear, listen to the sounds, groans and angst pronounced like an auctioneer and diminish them with love that comes only from facing them.

Spirit has guided me over and through the brambles of recovery from the disease of alcoholism. This Bridge game was one of the most humbling gifts I have received from Spirit in some time. Humbling, because I was embraced and encouraged with kindness and acceptance by the three women playing the game. Humbling because they liked *Me* and asked *Me* if I would come again when they needed a fill-in, a fourth hand at their weekly game. Spirit made use of my fear and their kindness to heal another wound. A wound that was keeping me from Spirit's Highest Good. Thank you, Peggy.

Walking

*I*WALKED THIS MORNING IN the brilliant fall sunshine, before the wind began blowing and the temperature soared to 94 degrees Fahrenheit. I've been in a bit of a funk, the kind that is like a low-grade fever—it slows you down, but doesn't stop you in your tracks. I call this mood "low-grade panic" because I function on autopilot.

Every spiritual teacher and counselor I've ever had and those I've studied encourage physical exercise as a positive and natural booster for emotional and physical energy. Research reveals the effect of exercise changes the level of beta-endorphins in the brain and the person's mood for the better. Well, I certainly wanted my mood to change this morning.

I hopped into my walking shoes, put on my sun visor and sunglasses and started walking. I felt like a large rock, my shoulders stooped and felt heavy, my stomach sagged and my head hung down. The first few minutes I just walked and then I began to breathe more deeply. I reminded myself to hold my head up and shoulders back and pull my stomach in to maximize my breathing and strengthen those flabby muscles.

Walking

I noticed the leaves on the cotton wood trees were beginning to change color, the sun had dipped lower, the sky was brilliant blue, and I had increased my walking speed. I began to swing my arms to the rhythm of my walking speed. I began to lose the sense of dread that had catapulted me into the walk in the first place.

My mind went from worry to gratitude. I began a list of gratitude, thanking Spirit for my healthy body, feet and legs that walk easily and effortlessly. I gave thanks for the money in my checking account, and money that was coming my way. I gave thanks for my loyal and loving friends and family—you know, those folks I was angry at before I began the walk. I gave thanks for my safe environment, the fall colors of brilliant orange and yellow and the love and trust I have in Spirit. Oh yes, my mood lifted, my heart opened and I was smiling by the time I walked the three miles.

Exercise of any kind is good for the mind and body. In the past, I used to faithfully spend an hour or so at the gym on the cardio machines, lifting weights, attending spin classes, Pilates classes, etc. These days I practice an exercise regime of walking and lifting weights at home. Walking helps me gain insight into the nature of my inner being and I feel connected to the Universe.

I have also learned to not think too much about exercise or walking. I just get up, put on my walking shoes and set a goal for the amount of time I will walk. Walking has changed my outlook on many problems and life challenges. I know it will do the same for you. Get up, pop into those walking shoes and walk.

Inspirations From Women

I INVITED WOMEN I ADMIRE to submit narratives about their happy lives. Below are several statements from women who answered my call.

Ellen Robertson Green, Dean of Communications and Marketing, Texas:

"Life is a constant stream of miracles. This mantra comforts me. Mother's prescription to recapture the brilliance and independence ripped from her by stroke provides insight. Shouldn't we all: quiet the brain, acknowledge and celebrate each small accomplishment, invite positive energy, reject the negative, work hard, accept help, welcome love?"

Jolanda Brady, dula and massage therapist, Florida:

"I have been practicing and am committed to listen to my feelings, my heart, soul, my inner voice, focusing on what brings me pleasure, what feels good, and to be open to receive. There has been quite some discomfort, and I know action takes courage, so I have made a commitment to myself to pave my road, my journey to my desires with pleasure, love, and courage, no matter how "tough" it sometimes seems to be, and living like that makes my light shine so much brighter in relationships, career, health, finances.

"Judith, I want you to know how much you have helped me, inspired me, to do what I'm currently doing now. I honor your presence in my life and I honor you with all the courageous actions you take—they are all mirrors, signs, messages for me..."

Mary Ann Boggess, entrepreneur and artist, Arkansas:
"All I ever wanted was to be happy. I learned that was up to me, no one else. I am so grateful that I have the ability to let go of those things that stand in the way of my happiness. Letting go is the most empowering thing that I can do."

Marianne Merritt Talbot, attorney and Goddess Extraordinaire, New York City:
"Living boldly in my life is about venturing on less-accepted (but always more adventurous) paths to follow my heart, principles, and conscience, sharing my truths with a strong and ringing voice, surrounding myself with beautiful things to keep me perpetually inspired (like chandeliers) and wearing really fabulous French red lipstick."

The best part of living a bold life requires only our commitment and desire to have the life we want. These four women have each faced life challenges, disappointments and curveballs that only life can throw. Rather than survive their life challenges, they have thrived and become even bolder and yes, louder.

Quick, do a mental check list of the bold areas of your life and how you have been inspired to go higher and be bolder. Commit to being bold and loud—let the flow of your desires begin.

October

*Creating physical movement
from the spiritual realm*

Right Outcomes Are Unfolding

WHAT OUTCOMES NEED TO unfold for you at this very minute? Before you read any further, get a sheet of paper and write down the challenges you are facing and the outcomes you desire. Not those outcomes someone has told you need to happen, but those outcomes you desire. Really, write them down now and return to this reading.

Okay, you've got your list in front of you. I've got my list also and I'll share it with you.

Challenges:
- Having my book published
- Repaying debts—house mortgage and car loan

My List of Desired Outcomes:
- My book is published and is number one on the New York Times Best Seller List
- Financial Freedom.

I felt over-burdened and overwhelmed when I wrote those two challenges. I felt hope and inspiration when I wrote the desired outcomes. The challenges are real and with my human disposition of fear and doubt, they seem insurmountable. The outcomes seem out of my reach and beyond my ability to make happen.

Jerry and Esther Hicks, spiritual teachers, teach the Principle of Focused Attention. This is a tool I use to create vibrational energy that draws a desired outcome into my reality. This principle says 17 seconds of focused thought is more powerful than 2,000 hours of action. Focus 17 seconds on the outcome—imagine in your mind's eye the outcome of your desire.

I write the outcome with a script and carry it with me to use whenever I have 17 seconds, 34 seconds, etc., to focus my attention on the outcome I desire. For instance, here is my book-publishing focus and script: "I am a published author. I am a highly sought after speaker for women's conferences and workshops. I am having fun and am making loads of money."

You've got your list of outcomes; now write a script describing the outcome. Focus for 17 seconds on saying the script. I focus with a smile, a light heartedness and joy. Go to my blog and share your script and outcome with me. Once it happens, share the results. I want to know if you got the house painted, paid off your mortgage, got the dream woman/man, traveled to Italy or got that perfect job.

The right outcomes unfold according to our focused intention. Positive intention draws positive outcome. Practice the 17 seconds of the Principle of Focused Attention every day, take the necessary actions to create

Right Outcomes Are Unfolding

the energy to bring about the outcome that you desire. Your desired outcomes are in the flow; hop in and enjoy the ride.

Action Is the Process; the Goal Is the Outcome

I HAVE READ MANY BOOKS giving detailed instructions for "creating desired outcomes." Following those instructions I have visualized the desired outcome, hoping and believing it would materialize. I have created vision boards by cutting out pictures, pasting them on a poster board and imagining my desired outcome, both mentally and physically. I have practiced the Law of Attraction, the Law of Focused Attention, Law of Prayer, etc. and hoped my desired outcomes would materialize.

One of my greatest character defects is believing other people have the answers to my life's mysteries—the mysteries of love, romance, prosperity, professional success, happy children, successful marriage or partnership, weight, on and on and on. I have read hundreds of books, spent thousands of dollars in therapy and prayed like a mad woman, hoping my desired outcomes would pop out of the hemisphere and I would be forever happy.

I know the visualizations and affirmations have power and assist in moving the outcome forward. However, there are two processes that must be implemented before

Action Is the Process; the Goal Is the Outcome

the imaging and affirming stirs the hemisphere to move toward our desires. Those two processes are *thoughts* and *actions*.

Thoughts reflect my belief. If I desire an outcome but believe it is out of my reach or that I am undeserving, that outcome will NEVER be fulfilled. I must believe I can achieve the outcome and then take the necessary actions to make it happen. Recently, I wanted to lose ten pounds. I would put on my favorite jeans and think "I need to lose ten pounds." And away I would go to lunch and eat a burger, knowing I wanted to lose ten pounds, and thinking "I'll start tomorrow." My thoughts and actions were not committed to the desired outcome.

On December 30th, 2009 I committed to three desired outcomes: buy a new car, lose ten pounds, sell my house and buy a townhouse. I bought the new car on December 30th, 2009. On January 3rd, 2010 I took action and joined Weight Watchers with my goal of losing ten pounds and I called a realtor and put my house on the market to sell. I committed to my thoughts of my desired outcomes and took new actions.

I attended the Weight Watchers' meetings and not only did I lose the ten pounds, I lost 17. I lost 17 pounds in eight months, basically two pounds a month. I liked the results from losing the ten pounds so much, I committed to losing six pounds more and lost seven more pounds. My favorite jeans went to Goodwill and now I am wearing a new pair of favorite jeans.

My house sold on April 30th, 2010. A first-time home buyer wanted to enjoy the tax credits and the contract was signed by buyer and seller at 10:30 P.M., one and a half hours before the deadline for the tax credits. I got really busy and found the perfect townhouse in just six days. May 6th, 2010 I signed the contract for the townhouse that I had written about in my journal.

All three of these outcomes took action. I had test driven new cars for five months before I bought my car on December 30th, 2009. The actions came after the thoughts and commitment to these three desires. Action is the process; the goal is the outcome.

You've read my desire to have a bestseller on the NY Times list—the only way that is going to happen is for me to write. I haven't written for two weeks because I was pissed I wasn't chosen as the Advice Guru for Good Morning America. I thought, what the hell—why write, why try to break out of the box of work I've been in for 30 years? It is just too damn hard, and I am never going to be published, much less be on the bestseller list.

Those thoughts have kept me stymied for 18 days. This morning I asked Spirit to reveal my true place with work and I began to write. My self-pity and fearful thinking had caused me to stop writing. Prayer is faith in action, and, with inspiration from Spirit, I took action, turned on my computer and began to write. I feel empowered, purposeful and believe in my book again. Different action, different thoughts.

What are your desired outcomes? Have you committed to them spiritually and physically? Do you believe you are worthy of these desires? Are they attainable? I encourage you to write them in a journal and date the

Action Is the Process; the Goal Is the Outcome

page. Write the most important steps for each outcome to materialize.

If negative thoughts are your enemy, then reframe them to positive thoughts. If this is a new process for you, then tackle the easiest desires first and become proficient in taking action with thoughts of success and completion.

This process is similar to the chicken or the egg riddle—new thoughts, new actions or new actions, new thoughts? The spark before the flame creates a lighted candle. Whatever the psychology is behind the movement, just get moving. Get that list of steps you wrote and start the active process to reach your goal. Look at me—17 pounds later with new jeans, driving a new car, living in a new townhouse, getting out of the familiar work rut and writing a book.

Action—take the action and the rest will follow.

Happiness

I WAS ASKED RECENTLY if I was happy, and my immediate reply was, "Yes." The next question asked was why was I happy. My reply, "Because I choose to be."

I have direct knowledge of my statement about choosing to be happy. Every morning upon awakening, thoughts begin. Some days my thoughts are filled with anticipation, excitement and creative ideas, and I pop out of bed and zip off to a great day. Some days my thoughts are like rocks that are so heavy and big, I can hardly move. I think about my bank account, the colleague at work who drives me crazy and the yard that needs mowing. Some days, I am neutral—not necessarily flat, just on hold, waiting for something to happen.

Marcus Aurelius, philosopher and Roman emperor, wrote, *"The happiness of your life depends upon the quality of your thoughts."* Another one of those statements that is easy to read, yet difficult to maneuver.

Nobody is happy all the time. Some folks are happy most of the time and some say they are seldom happy, but no one has ever claimed to be happy 100% of the time. The people I have found to be happy, contented,

Happiness

satisfied, fulfilled—there are many descriptors—live these simple yet profound goals in no particular order:

1. Choose happiness—literally, smile and say, "I choose to be happy." Did you notice a change in your heart rate, your facial expression? Make the conscious choice to be happy.

2. Exercise—turn on the music and dance. Wherever you are, start dancing. If you are in your car, turn up the music and start moving. Smile while you are dancing and you will enhance the endorphins even more. Go to the gym, walk around the neighborhood park, hit the ground and do 20 pushups. Move your body and notice the immediate effect.

3. Do something for another person—call a friend or even do something bigger: leave a $100 dollar bill anonymously in a friend's mailbox. I did that for a friend who was having financial issues and she called me and told me about her surprise. She might as well have won the lottery. It felt so good and worthwhile. To this day, I have never told her I was the giver.

Hug your spouse or child for no reason. Make their favorite dessert. Just writing this makes me feel better, so imagine how you will feel when you do it.

4. Save money—every month, put money in a savings account, even if it is only $10.00 or $100.00. Save something every month. When you are feeling overwhelmed, open up your account or savings book and see the numbers growing. Smart financial choices relieve stress.

5. Spend no less than 15 minutes a day alone. You

decide how you are going to do it. For some, it may be the commute in the car, if they are in traffic and not stressed. Some may spend the 15 minutes on a walk, in the bathroom or among the bookshelves at Barnes and Noble. I drink my first cup of coffee in bed every morning by myself. This is when I choose my thoughts for the day—I focus on the good in my life, I make a mental gratitude list, say a prayer to Spirit and when I finish that cup of coffee, I am usually fit for the day.

On the days I cannot shake off the gloom, I embrace the feeling and let it wash over me. I call my friend and give five minutes to the problem and then listen to her giving me easy suggestions of how to let go. Just sharing the not-so-perfect feelings gives me a sense of belonging. Sometimes, by mid-day my thoughts begin to change and I notice a connection to my inner self. The fog has lifted. I may not answer "Yes" to the question about being happy, but I am better.

My thoughts are either messages of hope or messages of despair. I often cannot change my thoughts without taking action. That is why I like to move my body—that old adage, "Move the body and the mind will follow" works for me.

In fact, I've been in a slump today. Writing this narrative was an action step that has lifted my spirits. While writing, I watched the video of Pink at the 2010 Grammys, "Glitter in the Air," and her amazing performance. If you haven't, find it and watch it on YouTube. Stand up and dance to the music and imagine flying high and happy.

Reality Check

WHY A REALITY CHECK? If you are like me and have an ego that spits out lies, deceit, drainage with spiders and a multitude of half truths, then a reality check may help. My reality begins with an early morning meditation. I particularly like Emmet Fox's books of metaphysical teachings. These books and their spiritual messages have inspired me for the moment, lasting into the day's activities.

This reality check meditation is for the now and the most worthy definition I know of NOW is "NOW spelled backwards is WON." If we can stay in the now, we have won. In order for me to do that I require a Reality Check: "an assessment to determine if my circumstances or expectations conform to reality." Well, that's a tall order when my life is on the line, when my love obsession hasn't returned my call, when my job is in jeopardy, when my loved one is ill with no diagnosis. I am not in the now with these life challenges and winning is the last thing on my mind.

I have learned that being in the now is profound. A spiritual mentor offered me a sound piece of advice in 1984 after I had called more than ten times in one day with the problem of the century. She said "Honey, I suggest you practice gratitude. Tell your Spirit 'thank you for my life exactly the way it is today.' " She said, "This may be as good as it gets for you and you are missing it." Ouch, that one hurt!

So, even though I didn't mean it (and by the way, the problem was a man), I said "Thank you for my life exactly the way it is today." A reality check. Yeah, I began a reality check. I asked myself, "Am I breathing?" Yes. "Is my rent paid?" Yes. "Do I have a job?" Yes. "Are the holes in my pantyhose visible to the public eye?" No. "Am I going to die if I don't hear from Joe?" I want to die, but I am not going to die.

Back in the now, back in reality, back in the moment and realizing my ego was once again lying to me. I began to breathe, I began to relax, and guess what—Joe called.

Bring yourself back to the now. Offer up the gratitude of your current reality and open your heart and get out of your head. Life is way more fun in reality than in the ego. It is certainly less dramatic.

November

The simplistic tool of gratitude

Be Grateful No Matter What

"If the only prayer you ever say in your entire life is thank you, it will be enough."
Meister Eckhart

DO YOU HAVE GRATITUDE for challenging circumstances in your life? Are you able to make a list of gratitudes easily and effortlessly? Do you want to use gratitude as a life tool that works? Is gratitude a daily attitude for you, or do you use it on the run or sly?

I believe gratitude can be used to make any situation better, bigger and more rewarding. I began practicing the concept of gratitude many years ago. I was full of dismay and despair, unhappy with my life, job, romantic partner, and wanted some relief. A friend I trusted, whose life looked like a life I wanted to emulate, taught me the tool of gratitude. We didn't discuss the definition of "gratitude" or even the outcomes I was demanding from the Universe. I was simply told to make a list of things I was grateful for in my life.

Being a novice at recognizing what I had to be grateful for, I was lead tenderly and carefully this first time. We started with the basics of food in the refrigerator, electricity working, apartment rent paid, car starting every morning, job and salary, healthy body and working limbs. This all seemed rather silly to me. I questioned the list, as everyone had these things. Why should I be grateful for the obvious? Oh, the wrong question to ask.

I was jerked up by my ungrateful Prada boot straps and told to look around me and realize many people would literally kill to have the life I lived. I had no worry, no wants and no uncertainty as to where I would sleep, what or if I would eat. I had health insurance, car insurance and a family who cared about me. I began to understand that gratitude was much bigger than my selfishness and inability to be grateful for what I had rather than what I was demanding.

From this initial lesson of gratitude I began to take baby steps. I learned how to make a decent gratitude list regarding the abundance in my life. I eventually learned how to use gratitude to release negative thinking by thanking the Universe for my life exactly the way it is, including those things I did not want in my life.

I have learned how to reframe the negative to the positive. I believe by changing my thoughts with grateful thinking I can change my circumstances. Years ago, when my second husband and I were separated, I literally had no money in my purse or bank account and it was five days to pay day. I was very worried but decided to practice this new tool of gratitude. I thanked Spirit on the way home from work for the food in my pantry, gas in my car, and the apples and oranges my mother had left on my counter.

Upon arriving home I went to the mailbox and there was a check for $75.00 from a local hospital. To this day I do not know why that check had been sent to me.

Be Grateful No Matter What

Standing at the mailbox, I cried. I immediately called a friend and asked if I should call the hospital to see if it was a mistake. She calmly but very firmly said, "No, just be grateful."

Did I change my circumstances by changing my thoughts? I don't know. The check would probably have been there without me giving thanks for what I had. But that experience spurs me on when my life is filled with fear and I do not know how scary circumstances are going to turn out. I make gratitude lists almost every day, if not on paper, then in my head when I am taking a shower, driving to work, on my daily walk, preparing dinner or sometimes as I lay my head on my pillow at the end of the day.

I believe gratitude opens doors that otherwise would stay closed or only slide partway open. Do you use gratitude? Does it work? Great, make a gratitude list right now—start at the beginning with the easy ones—sun shining, loving friends, healthy children. Now move into the hard stuff—the paycheck that doesn't seem to cover the monthly bills, the boss that is a jerk, the boyfriend or husband who is slow to appreciate you, the family that is a curse, the pimple on your nose the night before the presentation. Give thanks for your life exactly the way it is today.

The other gratitude list I make is one giving thanks in advance for those things yet to come that I either require or desire. I write at the top of the page, "'Thanks in advance for: the unknown source of money for the mortgage, the job that is rightfully mine, the invitation to

Italy with all expenses paid, the $300 for my contacts." This type of gratitude opens my mind to receive and be open to new opportunities that I otherwise might ignore. An attitude of gratitude is a magic jewel that brings about wonders we know not where from.

Why a Gratitude List?

HAVE YOU EVER HAD A DAY without complaining? A day when not one complaint came to your mind? A day when you felt an intense desire to be thankful for the most inane things in your life? Most of us have a combination of complaints and thankfulness throughout the day. I have learned that life is a series of ups and downs, wins and losses, successes and failures—every day offers an event for which I can complain or be grateful.

Complaining and discussing the wrongs that have been done to us has sometimes become a psychological check list required for personal growth. I'm not demeaning check lists; I am suggesting that complaining begets complaints. Being thankful begets thankfulness and more of the very thing we all want, and that is to feel whole, connected, appreciated, appealing, and at the very least, happy.

Most every self-improvement book, journal or workshop encourages using the spiritual concept of gratitude. In *The Power of the Word*, an essay by Florence Scovel Shinn, she states, *"Woman's only enemies are within herself."* Nothing on the outside has the power to actually hurt me. It's those negative, self-pitying, self-doubtful thoughts that cause me harm, because I believe them.

Most women answer the question, "What do you want?" by talking about what they don't want. Same with the question, "What are you grateful for?" Today I am impatiently waiting for an important phone call about my dream job. I am anxious about my security and future and have placed an inordinate sense of importance on the end result of the call. I can compile a massive list of complaints about waiting for the damn call. Instead, with the help of a gratitude list, I will examine the things that make the wait possible.

Listing those people, events, serendipities, even the timing in my life, my mindset changes from complaining to thankfulness; this entire year's events have lead me to this gratitude list. I am grateful for:

❊ the dead-end job that led me to realize and remember I am a powerhouse, a thunderstorm in the room

❊ networking and asking for help from women I trust and admire

❊ my age of 63 years. I have life experiences and circumstances that only now qualify me for the job in question. Woo hoo.

❊ perfect and elegant timing in my life. Florence Scovel Shinn says, *"Divine ideas never conflict, the call will come at the right time."*

❊ the women who have supported my desire for celebrity status, national recognition and financial independence.

Why a Gratitude List?

✸ these women's spiritual rituals, their prayers that are igniting the Universe and the decision makers who choose me for the job that is rightfully mine

✸ the intuitive feeling that the job was mine by Divine Right because of the timing of events leading to the notice of the job

✸ being able to conjure and absorb all that is rightfully mine

✸ the wait for the phone call—it offers the opportunity to balance me physically, mentally and spiritually.

Gratitude lists alter us spiritually. We become alert and take advantage of every opportunity that comes our way. One of the most powerful affirmations I know comes from Florence Scovel Shinn: *"Thy will be done this day. Today is a day of completion. I give thanks for this perfect day, miracle shall follow miracle and wonders shall never cease."*

As I have made gratitude a habit I have seen miracle after miracle and ceaseless wonders in my life. I haven't received the phone call yet but I feel a damn sight better, less anxious and more calm and poised. I believe that which is mine comes easily and effortlessly to me. I am grateful.

Begin to make a gratitude list and thank the Universe for the things that you are least grateful for today. Putting the list in writing makes the gratitude concrete and the energy spreads around the cosmos like fairy dust. I have had fairy dust sprinkled when I least expected it and my world would change in a flash.

Thanksgiving

"On Thanksgiving Day we acknowledge our dependence."
William Jennings Bryan

I LOVE THE TRADITION OF Thanksgiving Day. I try to maintain an attitude of gratitude every day and particularly on Thanksgiving Day, as this is a day when nothing is exchanged or required for participation.

Gathering folks around my dining room table for the traditional meal is such fun. As in most households, the menu consists of turkey, mashed garlic potatoes, dressing, gravy, cranberry sauce, green beans, tossed salad, pecan and pumpkin pies, and real whipped cream. I set the table with red table cloths, Friendly Village dishes given by my mother to her parents on their 50th wedding anniversary, silver and fresh flowers.

Living a bold life is never accomplished alone. Hundreds of people have shared their experiences, strength and hope with me. They have cheered me on when the race seemed endless. My parents wanted only the best for me and gave me more than I can ever repay. The bar was set for a college education and I accomplished that with their enthusiasm and financial support. Mother was a quiet force while my father's voice rang loud and clear with expectations for me.

Thanksgiving

My sisters and brother have invited me into their homes when I needed to be dependently independent. When I had no money for rent and wanted desperately to be on my own, my sister Joan, and my brother Joe, each invited me into their homes. The college semester I lived with Joe he gave me *carte blanche* with his checking account. Was he crazy? Maybe, but he loved me and shared his bachelor pad with the backyard swimming pool with me.

Every Thanksgiving I share my blessings bestowed on me by Spirit in these simple ways: I hand $10.00 to a single mom, serve dinner at a homeless shelter, invite single folks to dinner, deliver pecan pies on Thanksgiving eve to my favorite friends, give coats to the coat drive. I do this to express my gratitude for the life I live today. I believe gratitude in motion reaps benefits for both the giver and the receiver.

What will you do to express your gratitude? Make a list of ideas and take action.

Create Your Desires in Silence, Imagination and Gratitude

*I*BELIEVE OUR HEART'S desires are nudges from Spirit, a higher order or sphere. These are desires that nymphs and sirens sing in the gap from our heart to our thoughts to our actions. There are many practices to ignite these desires and I suggest you try the following if you are experiencing resistance to their being fulfilled.

1. Relax. Become silent and begin thinking on Spirit. A peace will pass over you. Feel the comfort and serenity of Spirit. Say to yourself "peace" as many times as necessary until you feel the serenity of the word. Force nothing. Relax, remain silent. Breathe. Focus on Spirit, repeat "peace" to yourself slowly and easily and let the feeling wash over you,

2. Once you relax (and that becomes easier as you practice), dwell only on the good. Claim perfection and repeat "Only good exists, at all times, under all circumstances, in spite of the contrary." Claim only perfection. "I see perfection."

3. Return to the silence, relax and breathe.

4. Breathe and state your desire. State it simply and

Create Your Desires in Silence, Imagination and Gratitude

directly. State it with feeling and as if it already exists. Say, "I see perfection: perfect Spirit, perfect woman, perfect desire (be very specific about naming the desire—if it is a job, say, "'I see my perfect job;" if it is financial freedom, say, "I see perfect financial freedom;" if it is a healing of some kind, say, "I see perfect healing").

❋ Imagine your desire being fulfilled. See yourself in reality with the fulfilled desire.

❋ Visualize a flower, a nature scene, a beautiful piece of art—use the power of visualization to stimulate the process. (Do not force this visualization, just let it happen.)

❋ Feel the desire, express joy and love in this feeling. Put joy in every thought and word about the desire—the joy of faith and assurance, the joy of knowing you are living your desire.

❋ Believe that your desire is being fulfilled easily, effortlessly and with perfect timing and grace. Bless everything with love. Hold love in every thought and word, in your mind and body. Love God and all those known and unknown.

5. Practice gratitude. Give thanks in the form of prayer. End your prayer in gratitude and say, "It is done." Do this every day, as many times as you can or feel the need and your reward will be rich.

6. Now go back and repeat #2 once more, claiming perfection. It is done.

December

The holidays

Christmas at My House

CHRISTMAS IS CELEBRATED around the world in many different ways and with many different customs. In many countries it is a public or national holiday and is commercial in nature. In North and South America, the United Kingdom and much of Europe, it is a widely celebrated holiday.

Christmas spending in the United States accounts for 40% of the annual sales for many retailers. Many holiday shoppers in the US hold out until the last minute for the best deal. Children still write letters to Santa Claus.

When I was a young child growing up in a family with five children, my parents strove to give each of us at least one fantasy gift. My mother loved Christmas and made the holidays as bright and beautiful as possible. We celebrated with outside decorations and lights, beautiful tree decorations and a major culinary production.

Mother would set the table with her pink china, silver and serving dishes she saved for special occasions. Her happiest Christmases were when all children and grandchildren would gather in her home for the holiday. Food was and is a dynamic component of our family's love for each other, no matter the holiday.

The Age of Sage

Christmas dinner consisted of bone-in ham, green beans, mashed potatoes, homemade yeast rolls, salad with Mother's famous blue cheese dressing and relish trays. Both my mother and father were excellent cooks and bakers. Mother made pie crust from scratch and Daddy made mincemeat for pies. Mother used real whipped cream to plop on top of the mincemeat, pecan and pumpkin pies.

Gifts came after the meal, and as our family was so large, we drew names to offset the cost of buying for over 16 people. When I was younger the day was all about the gifts. Today the gift is being with my family and the circle of love my mother had created and passed on to her children.

My celebration of Christmas is so different today than when I was younger. I go to my family's annual gathering a weekend before Christmas, usually at my brother's home in Shamrock, Texas. My parents are dead, so we all share the cooking now. Several years ago we decided to not draw names for gifts and instead bring a "gag" or "glad" gift valued at no more than $20.00. We have played this gift game before and it turns into a free-for-all with lots of laughter and excitement as we each go about trying to steal the gift that we really want from each other.

I detest the commercial message of Christmas. Those Hallmark advertisements should be banned from television. The message I hear is, "There is something wrong with me if I am not with the one I love or don't receive the gift of my dreams."

To celebrate the meaning of giving during Christmas, I donate money in the names of friends and family to local charities. I send money to friends who struggle financially. On Christmas day I prepare dinner for my single friends who would otherwise be alone. Sharing this day with others gives me a sense of hope and that I am doing my part for humanity.

I prepare a Northern New Mexico Christmas feast of green chili, tamales, *posole* and *biscochitos*, the New Mexico State cookie. After our meal, I ask each guest to state a desire for the approaching year.

Whatever you do to celebrate Christmas, do it with joy and happiness. At the end of the day when my dinner guests are gone, the dishes are done, the table and chairs have been reset, I feel a joy and a connection with Spirit that no other gift provides.

The Most Extraordinary Gift

YOU MAY HAVE A LOVING home, loving relationship, loving family—love may come easily and effortlessly and every day of your life, including the holidays; holidays might be all about love for you. If that is true, good for you, put down this book and hug your loved ones. If it isn't true for you and you are worrying about how to handle holidays, then read on.

In the past the angst used to begin for me on November 1st and continued through January 2nd. I understand today that the angst came from unrealistic expectations of those 60 days, and quite frankly, I grew tired of being sad and depressed. Who in this world, your world, any world, has everything they want? You may be married and feel lonelier than I. You may be alone and dancing on the ceiling.

Whatever your circumstance, there are many ways to feel the love you so strongly desire and deserve. The gifts below are things you can give freely. Some are actually free and some may cost a bit, but each will express love and appreciation to the receiver.

Extraordinary Gifts of Love

Babysit for a friend while they Christmas shop.
Cook a meal for a friend just because you love them.
Wrap presents for a friend.
Help someone decorate their Christmas tree.
Invite those who are alone to your home for Christmas.
Give a treasure you no longer use to someone.
Send a holiday card to someone you don't particularly like.
Pay $5.00 for the person behind you in the express line.
Give your time. Give your understanding and compassion.
Give encouragement to the least likely person.
Leave a Benjamin Franklin bill in an unmarked envelope in a deserving friend's mailbox.

There are ways to give gifts that celebrate the season and express your love toward the people around you without costing you anything. Get busy to see what you can find that's free. Then, turn right around and give it to someone else. The love you express will remain in the receiver's heart forever. And, oh my, how you will glow like a Christmas light as your love comes pouring forth through your extraordinary gifts.

May your Christmas be bright and filled with the love for you and from you.

All I Want For Christmas

PEACE IN MY WORLD and the world at large.
Laughter and a big guffaw every day of the year.
An invitation to dance on Dancing With the Stars.
Financial freedom.

An all-expense-paid international travel invitation.

Continued excellent health.

Dinner with Charlie Rose—I have a crush on Charlie and desire to dine with him in NYC.

Holiday in the Caribbean at the Sandpiper five-star hotel.

Dallas Cowboys to win a Super Bowl.

A phone call from my latest flaming romance.

Romance and love. A passionate, fun, flirty, intelligent, wealthy and well-read man whose eyes and heart are only for me.

A big blue box from Tiffany's on 5th Avenue with shiny surprises.

A stroll down 5th Avenue NYC on my lover's arm as we laugh and flirt through the crowds.

A massage/spa gift of 52 massages for the 52 weeks in the year.

Monthly speaking engagements that provide a six-figure income.

The Gift That Keeps on Giving

THE GIFT THAT KEEPS ON GIVING is a big box of love. Can you imagine a beautifully wrapped package of red foil paper, with green and gold tinsel ribbon, anticipating a fabulous gift and out pops love? Love, that eternal gift of joy, gratitude, comfort, companionship, peace, laughter is the one thing that each of us desires and does not ask for without fear of rejection.

When I was a sophomore in high school my mother sewed two skirts for me for Christmas—one orange and red tweed, and one blue and grey wool with perfect pleats. Mother bought a gorgeous orange sweater for the tweed skirt and a grey sweater for the pleated skirt. Everything my mother did was done with love.

Our family of seven lived on two public school teachers' salaries. Money was tight and used mostly for necessities. Mother wanted each of us to have a gift that would make us feel unique and special. Mother was a self-taught seamstress and making the skirts at a small cost allowed her to buy the two sweaters to complement the skirts and complete this lavish gift for me. I don't remember what my brother and sisters received, but I am sure their gifts were as special to them as mine were to me.

This particular Christmas past stands out for me as one of a big box of love—the gift that keeps on giving. The memory of my mother's love warms me today and is the catalyst for me to share my bounty with others. I have no children, no husband or lover today, no invitations from my sisters or brother to spend Christmas with them. So what can I do to create a Christmas of joy for me?

After years of the traditional meal at Christmas, the past several Christmases I have ventured into the spirit of Mexico and prepared green chili stew, tamales and a sundry of other delights. I use beautiful red tablecloths, candles and fine dining paper goods for my table. This year the fireplace will have a roaring fire and the spirit of Christmas will permeate my home, my guests and me.

What are you waiting for? Open your heart and home to folks just like you. If you have a family, express loving kindness and gratitude for their gift of love. You may even receive a gift that keeps on giving.

For the Fun of It!

EAT WHOLE GRAINS AND FIVE servings of fruit and vegetables every day.

Celebrate your birthday even if you are alone.

Dance to the music.

Always have a friend who is 20 years older.

Always have a friend who is 20 years younger.

Go to a movie alone and eat all the popcorn you want.

Invite a friend to the movie and share your popcorn.

Wear red lipstick.

Smile and flirt with the most unlikely man or woman.

Leave well enough alone.

For one month, buy only necessities.

Schedule a massage for your best friend.

Schedule a massage for yourself.

Dare to live your dreams—life is very short after 50.

Laugh at yourself every day.

Never laugh when someone is hurt until they begin to laugh.

Trust Spirit to guide and direct you—read something inspiring every day.

Teach your children to give to others who are less fortunate.

Unleash the goddess within and love at least once with total abandon.

Be sassy and sexy for yourself—wear red lacy underwear and enjoy the view!

The difference between a rut and a grave is the dimension.